I NEED A COPY OF THAT

COLLECTED BY
DAVID C. POWELL, M.D.

ↄ⏐ⱷ

Cork Hill Press
Indianapolis

CORK HILL PRESS™

Cork Hill Press
7520 East 88th Place, Suite 101
Indianapolis, Indiana 46256-1253
1-866-688-BOOK
www.corkhillpress.com

Trade Paperback Edition: 1-59408-233-2

Printed in the United States of America

1 3 5 7 9 10 8 6 4 2

INTRODUCTION

It is often said that laughter is the best medicine. Well, I believe they are correct (whoever "they" are). As a physician, I have dispensed, and received when needed, both big and small doses of real medicine. However, it is these small doses of humor, we all receive from time to time, on which this project was founded.

The seed for this project was planted when, as a fledgling surgeon at the University of Kentucky, I began collecting these bits of humor. How many times I have uttered, "I need a copy of that..." Over many years, the seed and dream of collecting and publishing these bits of humor has germinated and flourished into this current project. We all see these bit and pieces in our offices, on our computers, at the nursing stations and yes, even in the operating rooms. But what has happened to them? — thrown away, misplaced or forgotten.

Certainly in the post 9-11 days, we need the laughter more than ever. They are here; twenty-five years of the best of "I need a copy of that." Here are compiled the blondes, rednecks, lawyers and thoughts that make you go hmmm...Please enjoy, smile, laugh and if you indeed have some laying around, please send them in — "I need a copy of that..."

Disclaimer

Although rigorous attempts have been made in the evolution of this project to identify the sources of much of this material, it has been next to impossible to track down their genesis. As this material has been gathered on pieces of paper, sheets handed out at office meetings and e-mail forwards for over 25 years, there have been no identifiable authors authenticated for any of this material. All apologies to anyone inadvertantly slighted.

p.s. Who does own the "blonde" jokes?

Chapter I

MEDICINE HAS A FUNNY SIDE (?)

OR

LEARN HOW TO COOK, MARRY A DOCTOR!

The following quotes were taken from actual medical records as dictated by physicians...

- By the time he was admitted, his rapid heart had stopped, and he was feeling better.

- Patient has chest pain if she lies on her left side for over a year.

- On the second day, the knee was better and on the third day it had completely disappeared.

- She has had no rigors or shaking chills, but her husband states she was very hot in bed last night.

- The patient has been depressed ever since she began seeing me in 1983.

- Patient was released to outpatient department without dressing.

- I have suggested that he loosen his pants before standing, and then, when he stands with the help of this wife, they should fall to the floor.

- The patient is tearful and crying constantly. She also appears to be depressed.

- Discharge status: Alive but without permission.

- The patient will need disposition, and therefore we will get Dr. Blank to dispose of him.

- Healthy appearing decrepit 69 year old male, mentally alert but forgetful.

- The patient refused an autopsy.

- The patient has no past history of suicides.

- The patient expired on the floor uneventfully.

- Patient has left his white blood cells at another hospital.

- The patient's past medical history has been remarkably insignificant with only a 40 pound weight gain the past three days.

- She slipped on the ice and apparently her legs went in separate directions in early December.

- The patient experienced sudden onset of severe shortness of breath with a picture of acute pulmonary edema at home while having sex which gradually deteriorated in the emergency room.

- The patient had waffles for breakfast and anorexia for lunch.

- Between you and me, we ought to be able to get this lady pregnant.

- The patient was in his usual state of good health until his airplane ran out of gas and crashed.

- Since she can't get pregnant with her husband, I thought you would like to work her up.

- She is numb from her toes down.

- While in the ER, she was examined, X-rated and sent home.

- The skin was moist and dry.

- Occasional, constant, infrequent headaches. .

- Coming from Detroit, this man has no children.

- Patient was alert and unresponsive.

- When she fainted, her eyes rolled around the room.

What doctors say, and what they're really thinking:

- "This should be taken care of right away." (I'd planned a trip to Hawaii next month, but this is so easy and profitable that I want to fix it before it cures itself.)

- "Wellllllll, what have we here....?" (He has no idea and is hoping you'll give him a clue.)

- "Let me check your medical history." (I want to see if you've paid your last bill before spending any more time with you.

- "Why don't we make another appointment later in the week." (I'm playing golf this afternoon, and this is a waste of time – or – I need the bucks, so I'm charging you for another office visit.)

- "Let's see how it develops." (Maybe in a few days it will grow into something that can be cured.)

- "Let me schedule you for some tests." (I have a forty percent interest in the lab.)

- "I'd like to have my associate look at you." (He's going through a messy divorce and owes me a bundle.)

- "I'd like to prescribe a new drug." (I'm writing a paper and would like to use you for the guinea pig."

- "If it doesn't clear up in a week, give me a call." (I don't know what it is; maybe it will go away by itself.)

- "That's quite a nasty looking wound." (I think I'm going to throw up.)

- "This may smart a little." (Last week two patients bit off their tongues.)

- "Well, we're not feeling so well today, are we....?" (I'm stalling for time. Who are you and why are you here?)

- "This should fix you up." (The drug company slipped me some big bucks to prescribe this stuff.)

- "Everything seems to be normal." (Rats! I guess I can't buy that new beach condo after all.)

- "I'd like to run some more tests." (I can't figure out what's wrong. Maybe the kid in the lab can solve this one.)

- "Do you suppose all this stress could be affecting your nerves?" (You're crazier'n a outhouse rat. Now, if I can only find a shrink who'll split fees with me....)

- "There is a lot of that going around." (My God, that's the third one this week. I'd better learn something about this.)

- "If those symptoms persist, call for an appointment." (I've never heard of anything so disgusting. Thank God, I'm off next week.)

Mammogram Prep 101:

"I'm thinking of going to the doctor soon for my very first mammogram. I'm a little nervous about this... Is there anything that I can do to prepare?"

Mammograms require your breast to go gymnastic. If you have extremely agile breasts, you should do fine. Most breasts however, pretty much hang around doing nothing in particular, so they are woefully unprepared.

But you can prepare for a mammogram right at home using these simple exercises:

EXERCISE 1: Refrigerate two bookends overnight. Lay one of your breasts (either will do) between the two bookends and smash the bookends together as hard as you can. Repeat three times daily.

EXERCISE 2: Locate a pasta maker or old wringer washer. Feed the breast into the machine and start cranking. Repeat twice daily.

EXERCISE 3: (Advanced) Situate yourself comfortably on your side on the garage floor. Place one of your breasts snugly behind the rear tire of the family van. When you give the signal, hubby will slowly ease the van into reverse. Hold for five seconds. Repeat on the other side.

Doctors And Contributions

When doctors were told to contribute to the construction of a new wing at a hospital:

- The allergists voted to scratch it.

- The dermatologists preferred no rash moves.

- The gastroenterologists had a gut feeling about it.

- The micro surgeons were thinking along the same vein.

- The neurologists thought the administration had a lot of nerve.

- The obstetricians stated they were laboring under a misconception.

- The ophthalmologists considered the idea short-sighted.

- The orthopedists issued a joint resolution.

- The parasitologists said, "Well, if you encyst".

- The pathologists yelled, "Over my dead body!"

- The pediatricians said, "Grow up".

- The proctologists said, "We are in arrears".

- The psychiatrists thought it was madness.

- The surgeons decided to wash their hands of the whole thing.

- The radiologists could see right through it.

- The internists thought it was a hard pill to swallow.

- The plastic surgeons said, "This puts a whole new face on the matter".

- The podiatrists thought it was a big step forward.

- The <D.O.S> thought they were being manipulated.

And We Wonder Why!

God populated the earth with broccoli and cauliflower and spinach, green and yellow and red vegetables of all kinds, so Man and Woman would live long and healthy lives.

Then using God's great gifts, Satan created Ben and Jerry's and Krispy Crème. And Satan said, "You want chocolate with that?" And Man said "Yeah!" And Woman said, "And another one with sprinkles." And they gained 10 pounds.

And God created the healthful yogurt that Woman might keep the figure that Man found so fair.

And Satan brought forth white flour from the wheat, and sugar from the cane, and combined them. And Woman went from size 2 to size 6.

So God said, "Try my fresh green salad."

And Satan presented Thousand-Island Dressing and garlic toast on the side. And Man and Woman unfastened their belts following the repast.

God then said, "I have sent you heart healthy vegetables and olive oil in which to cook them."

And Satan brought forth deep fried fish and chicken-fried steak so big it needed its own platter. And Man gained more weight and his cholesterol went through the roof.

God then brought running shoes so that his children might loose those extra pounds.

And Satan gave cable TV with a remote control so Man would not have to toil changing the channels. And Man and Woman laughed and cried before the flickering light and gained pounds.

Then God brought forth the potato, naturally low in fat and brimming with nutrition.

And Satan peeled off the healthful skin and sliced the starchy center into chips and deep-fried them. And Man gained pounds.

God then gave lean beef so that Man might consume fewer calories and still satisfy his appetite.

And Satan created McDonald's and it's 99-cent double cheeseburger. Then said, "You want fries with that?" And Man replied, "Yea! And super size 'em." And Satan said "It is good."

And Man went into cardiac arrest.
God sighed and created quadruple bypass surgery.

And then Satan created HMOs!

New HMO Guidelines / Hospital Costs

In an effort to reduce costs this year, the following are effective immediately. Please share this information with your patients and physicians as soon as possible.

1) This hospital will no longer provide security. Each Charge Nurse will be issued a .38 caliber revolver and 12 rounds of ammunition. An additional 12 rounds will be stored in the pharmacy. In addition to routine nursing duties, Charge Nurses will patrol the hospital grounds 3 times each shift. In light of the similarity of monitoring equipment, the Critical Care Units will now assume security surveillance duties. The Unit Secretary will be responsible for watching cardiac and security monitors, as well as continuing previous secretarial duties.

2) Food service will be discontinued immediately. Patients wishing to eat will want to get their families to bring them a

brown bag meal, or you may make your own arrangements with Subway, Dominoes, etc. Coin-operated telephones will be available in patient rooms for this purpose.

3) Our telephone operators have all been let go, so if you are walking through the lobby and hear the telephone ringing, please answer it.

4) We have found it necessary to make substantial reductions in our transport team so we ask the cooperation of all patients. One transporter will take at least six patients in wheelchairs at a time to Radiology, PT, and other services. Please form a "train" by holding tightly on to the handles of the wheelchair in front of you.

5) Our Emergency room is really busy from 3:00 PM to 11:00 PM, so if you can please have your accidents and heart attacks in the mornings or early afternoons, that would really help to reduce your wait.

6) To expedite surgery cases, all A.M. admits and outpatient surgery patients are asked to be at the hospital 3 hours prior to surgery. Go to Central Sterile Supply, pick up a clean instrument tray and surgery pack and proceed to the Surgery Holding area. To help us reduce drug costs, please take several Aleve prior to arriving at the hospital for surgery.

7) Patients anticipating the need for a bedpan can check one out in the gift shop. They will be available in a wide variety of colors and styles to meet the aesthetic and physical requirements of our patients. A deposit will be required but is fully refundable if bedpan is returned clean.

8) To reduce patients' lengths of stay, nurses will have a choice of using in-line skates or skateboards. To expedite re-

sponse to patients' needs and discharges, nurse call systems will be modified and will be wired to a collar worn by nurses, which will deliver a mild shock when pushed by the patient.

9) Taking a cue from the airlines, Respiratory Therapists will be replaced by oxygen masks which will, should the need arise, automatically drop from the ceiling over patient beds. If this occurs, please place the mask over your nose and mouth and breathe normally.

10) The hospital got a real sweet deal on surplus white waiter's jackets and these will be issued to all physicians. Doctors, we apologize in advance because the jackets already had a first name embroidered on the pocket. We will work with you to find a name that you can live with. If you also are on the staff at the University Hospital, we hope this won't be a problem. We recognize that in academic settings, "length of coat status" is very important.

11) All first time moms are asked to volunteer to help out on the pediatrics floor — not only will this reduce hospital costs, but it will give you a much needed experience and a dose of reality after ogling over your own precious sleeping bundle of joy.

12) Housekeeping and physical therapy are combined. Mops will be issued to those patients who are ambulatory, thus providing range-of-motion exercises as well as a clean environment. Family members and friends of patients and ambulatory patients may also sign up to clean public areas to receive special discounts on their final bills. Time cards will be provided.

13) Plant Operations and Engineering are being eliminated. The hospital has subscribed to the TIME-LIFE "How to ...." Series of maintenance books. These books can be checked

out from Administration and the toolbox will be standard equipment on all nursing units. We will be receiving the series at a rate of one volume every other month. We already have the volume on Basic Wiring, but if a non-electrical problem occurs, please try to handle it as best you can until the appropriate volume arrives.

14) Cutbacks in the phlebotomy staff will be accommodated by only performing blood related lab tests on patients who are already bleeding.

15) Physicians will be informed that they may order no more than two X-rays per patient stay. This is due to the turn-around time required by Walgreen's Photo Lab. Two prints will be provided for the price of one and physicians are being advised to clip coupons from the Sunday paper if they want extra sets. Walgreen's will honor all competitors' coupons for one-hour processing in emergency situations, so if you come across coupons from other vendors, please clip them and send them to the Emergency Department.

16) In light of the extremely hot summer temperature and the high A/C bills that we received last summer, our new policy is to have fans available for sale or lease in the hospital gift shop. For those patients who do not wish to use electric fans, the old reliable hand held cardboard fans on a stick are free upon request.

17) The cost of hospital gowns continues to escalate so patients are asked to bring their own pajama top which nurses will be happy to slit up the back for you. Pajama bottoms are not permitted on patient units.

18) On the way to the hospital, please stop by Target or Wal-Mart and pick up two sets of twin bed sheets. Should you require extra linens during your stay, coin-operated washers and dryers are available for patient use.

19) Administration is assuming responsibility for grounds keeping duties. If an Administrator cannot be reached by calling the Administrative Office, it is suggested that you walk outside and listen for the sound of a lawn mower, weedwhacker, etc.

20) In addition to the current recycling programs, a bin for the collection of unused fruit and bread will soon be provided on each floor. Families, patients, and the few remaining staff are encouraged to contribute discarded produce. The resulting moldy compost will be utilized by the pharmacy for nosocomial production of antibiotics. These antibiotics will be available for purchase through the hospital pharmacy, and will coincidentally, soon be the only antibiotics listed in the hospital's formulary.

21) All patients scheduled for a mammogram are to stop first at "Hooters" for a preliminary check out.

22) If you have any questions regarding these cost cutting measures, please let us know. Thank you for your cooperation.

The Top Ten Signs You've Joined a Cheap HMO:

#10 Your annual breast exam is conducted at Hooters.

#9 Directions to your doctor's office include, "take a left when you enter the trailer park."

#8 The tongue depressors taste faintly of Fudgesicles.

#7 The only proctologist in the plan is "Gus" from Roto-Rooter.

#6 The only items listed under Preventive Care coverage is "an apple a day."

#5   Your "primary care physician" is wearing the pants you gave to Goodwill last month.

#4   "The patient is responsible for 200% of out-of-network charges" is not a typo.

#3   The only expense covered 100% is embalming.

#2   With your last HMO, your Prozac didn't come in different colors with little "M"s on them.

       And the Number One (#1) sign that you've joined a cheap HMO ....

#1   You ask for Viagra, you get a Popsicle stick and duct tape.

And Again, You Have A Cheap HMO If ....

1)   Pedal-powered dialysis machines.

2)   Use of antibiotics deemed an "unauthorized experimental procedure".

3)   Head-wound victim in the waiting room is on the last chapter of "War and Peace".

4)   Exam room has a tip jar ! ! !

5)   You swear you saw salad tongs and a crab fork on the instrument tray just before the anesthesia kicked in.

6)   "Will you be paying in eggs or pelts?"

7)   Tight budget prevents acquisition of separate rectal thermometers.

8) "Take two leeches and call me in the morning ! "

9) The company logo features a hand squeezing blood from a turnip.

10) Covered post-natal care consists of leaving your baby on Mia Farrow's doorstep.

11) Radiation treatment for cancer patients requires them to walk around with a postcard from Chernobyl in their pocket.

12) "Prenatal Vitamin" prescription is a box of "Tic-Tacs".

13) Chief surgeon graduated from University of "Benihana".

14) Doctor listens to your heart through a paper towel tube.

15) Plan covers only "group" gynecological exams.

16) Pre-printed script pads that say "WALK IT OFF, CANDY ASS ! ! "

17) To avoid a time consuming and expensive throat culture, the doctor just French kisses you.

18) Recycled bandages.

19) You can get flu shot "as soon as the hypodermic needle is dry".

20) Twenty-four hour claims line is 1-800-TUF-LUCK.

21) Costly MRI equipment efficiently replaced by an over-sized 2-sided copier.

22) Only participating physicians are Dr. Fine, Dr. Howard, Dr. Fine.

23)　　Enema ???? The lavatory faucet swivels to face upward ! ! ! !

HMO Humor:

Q:　What does HMO stand for?

A:　This is actually a variation of the phrase, "Hey, Moe". Its roots go back to a concept pioneered by Doctor Moe Howard, who discovered that a patient could be made to forget about the pain in his foot if he were poked hard enough in the eyes. Modern practice replaces the physical finger poke with hi-tech equivalents such as voice mail and referral slips, but the result remains the same.

Q:　Do all diagnostic procedures require pre-certification?

A:　No, only those you need.

Q:　I just joined a new HMO. How difficult will it be to choose the doctor I want?

A:　Just slightly more difficult than choosing your parents. Your insurer will provide you with a book listing all the doctors who were participating in the plan at the time the information was gathered. These doctors basically fall into two categories: those who are no longer accepting new patients, and those who will see you but are no longer part of the plan. But don't worry, the remaining doctor who is still in the plan and accepting new patients has an office just a half day's drive away.

Q:　What are pre-existing conditions?

A:　This is a phrase used by the grammatically challenged when they want to talk about existing conditions. Unfortunately, we appear to be pre-stuck with it!

Q:　Well, can I get coverage for my pre-existing conditions?

A:　Certainly, as long as they don't require any treatment.

Q: What happens if I want to try alternative forms of medicine?

A   You'll need to find alternative forms of payment!

Q: My pharmacy plan only covers generic drugs, but I need the name brand. I tried the generic medication, but it gave me a stomach ache. What should I do?

A: Poke yourself in the eye.

Q: I have an 80/20 plan with a $200 deductible and a $2,000 yearly cap. My insurer reimbursed the doctor for my outpatient surgery but I'd already paid my bill, What should I do?

A: You have two choices. Your doctor can sign the reimbursement check over to you, or you can ask him to invest the money for you in one of those great offers that only doctors and dentists hear about, like windmill farms or frog hatcheries.

Q: What should I do if I get sick while traveling?

A: Try sitting in a different part of the bus.

Q: No, I mean what if I'm away from home and I get sick?

A: You really shouldn't do that. You'll have a hard time seeing your primary care physician. It's best to wait until you return, and then get sick.

Q: I think I need to see a specialist, but my doctor insists he can handle my problem. Can a general practitioner really perform a heart transplant right in his office?

A: Hard to say, but considering that all you're out is the $10 co-payment, there's no harm giving him a shot at it.

"Doctor, I have an Ear Ache"

2000 B.C. – "Here, eat this root."

1000 B.C. – "That root is heathen, say this prayer."

1850 A.D. – "That prayer is superstition, drink this potion."

1940 A.D. – "That potion is snake oil, swallow this pill."
1985 A.D. – "That pill is ineffective, take this antibiotic."
1000 A.D. – "That antibiotic is artificial, Here, eat this root . . . . ."

Hillbilly Medical Terms

Benign .... What you be after you be eight.

Bacteria .... Back door to cafeteria.

Barium .... What you do with dead folks.

Cesarean Section .... A neighborhood in Rome.

Cat scan .... Searching for the cat.
Cauterize .... Made eye contact with her.

Colic .... A sheep dog.

Coma .... A punctuation mark.

D & C .... Where Washington is.

Dilate .... To live longer than your kids do.

Enema .... Not a friend.

Fester .... Quicker than someone else.

Fibula .... A small lie.

G. I. Series .... World Series of military baseball.

Genital... Non-Jewish person.

Hangnail .... What you hang your coat on.

Hospital .... The biggest building in town, other than Joe's Feed Warehouse or Frank's Lumber Mill.

Impotent .... Distinguished, well known.

Labor Pain .... Getting hurt at work.

Medical Staff .... A doctor's cane, sometimes shown with a snake.

Morbid .... A higher offer than I bid.

Nitrates .... Cheaper than day rates.

Node .... I knew it.

Outpatient .... A person who has fainted.

Pap Smear .... A fatherhood test.

Pelvis .... Second cousin to Elvis.

Post Operative .... A letter carrier.

Recovery Room .... Place to do upholstery.

Rectum.. Damn near killed him.

Secretion .... Hiding something.

Seizure .... Roman emperor who lived in the Cesarean Section.

Tablet .... A small table to change babies on.

Terminal Illness .... Getting sick at the train station.

Tumor .... More than one.

Urine .... Opposite of mine.

Varicose .... Near by.

Things You Don't Want to Hear During Surgery

1) Better save that. We'll need it for the autopsy.

2) Someone call the janitor, we're going to need a mop.

3) Wait a minute, if this is his spleen, then what's that?

4) Hand me that ...uh....that uh ....."thingie".

5)   OOPS! Hey, has anyone ever survived 500ml of this stuff before?

6)   Rats, there go the lights again .....

7)   Ya know, there's big money in kidneys. Heck, the guy's got two of 'em.

8)   Everybody stand back! I lost my contact lens!

9)   Could you stop that thing from beating? It's throwing my concentration off!

10) What's this doing here?

11) That's cool! Now can you make his leg twitch?!!

12) I wish I hadn't forgotten my glasses.

13) Well, folks, this will be an experiment for all of us.

14) Anyone see where I left that scalpel?

15) OK, now take a picture from this angle. This is truly a freak of nature.

16) Nurse, did this patient sign the organ donation card?

17) Don't worry, I think it is sharp enough.

18) She's gonna blow! Everyone take cover ! ! ! !

19) Rats! Page 47 of the manual is missing!

More Medical Terms:

Antibody	Against everyone
Artery	The study of fine paintings
Cardiac Arrest	Taken into custody after stealing a Coupe Deville
Cardiology Advance	Study of poker playing
Charlie Horse	A 10 to 1 long-shot in the Kentucky Derby
Congenital	Friendly
Genes	What you wear cutting grass
Organic	An organ work repairman
Paralyze	Too far fetched stories
Pharmacist	A person who makes a living in agriculture
Protein	In favor of young people
Scalpel	What you stand on to clean windows in high rise buildings.
Vein...	Conceited

You <u>Might</u> be a Nurse if.......

- You believe the first thing a person does when they enter this world, and the last thing they do before they leave it, is take a really big crap.

- You know what a 3-H enema is .... High, Hot, and Hell of a lot.

- You consider a tongue depressor an eating utensil.

- Your friends drag you to a strip bar after work to loosen you up. The young lady on stage does a nude spread eagle back bend with pelvic thrusts a foot and a half from your nose. You are not aroused, but you DO think, "I could catheterize that". (True story)

- You have ever tried to identify what a patient ate last by examining the barf on your shoes.

- You've ever basted your Thanksgiving turkey with a Toomey syringe!

- You have placed your irritating patients/family members on P.I.T.A. (Pain In The Ass) precautions!

- You're at the grocery store, look down and notice you have at least 2 body fluids on your shoes and it doesn't bother you.

- Ever told a confused patient your name was that of your coworker and to HOLLER if they need help.

- Ever referred to KY jelly as "Goober Grease".

- Ever passed on the green stuff at the buffet because you are certain you suctioned it from a patient earlier.

- You know it's a full moon without having to look at the sky.

- You have ever referred to a patient as "genetically exclusive" or "genetically challenged".

- You've developed a crease between your brows from tying NOT to inhale the various human secretions you've encountered over the years.

- You believe eating microwave popcorn out of a clean bed-pan is perfectly natural.

- You believe Tylenol, Advil, or Excedrin provides a large part of your daily calorie intake requirements.

- When checking the level of orientation of a patient, you aren't sure of the answer.

- You've ever pretended to sneeze and at the same time thrown KY jelly on a coworker's sleeve to make them think they got shot with a hocker.

- You've ever held a 14-gauge needle over someone's vein and said, "Now you're going to feel a little stick."

- You've ever sworn you're going to have "NO CODE" tat-tooed to your chest.

- You refer to motorcyclists as organ donors.
- You've ever had a patient with a nose ring, a brow ring, and twelve earrings say, "I'm afraid of shots."

- You stare at someone in utter disbelief when they actually cover their mouth to cough.

- You have a patient in four-point leathers that asks if you're a nurse and you reply "Yes", and walk away.

- A trained physician can't recognize the proper anatomy of a female for a catheter, but you get it on the first try.

- You believe that all bleeding stops .... Eventually.

- You think "awake and stupid" is an appropriate choice for mental status.

- You hate working the night of a full moon.

- You believe in the aerial spraying of Prozac.

- Discussing dismemberment over a meal seems perfectly normal.

- You believe the government should require a permit to reproduce.

- You plan your next meal while performing gastric lavage.

- You believe every waiting room should have a Valium salt lick.

- You believe you have patients who are demonically possessed.

- You refer to vegetable and you don't mean the food group.

- You believe the lab should have a "dumb shit" profile on the lab requisition.
- You have handled several "lost condom" cases.

- You firmly believe that "too stupid to live" should be a diagnosis.

- You have to leave the patient before you begin to laugh uncontrollably.

- You believe a book entitled "Suicide. Getting it Right the First Time" will be your next project.

- You find humor in other people's stupidity.

- You believe that 90% of people are a poor excuse for protoplasm.

- Your idea of fine dining is sitting down to eat.

- You believe chocolate is a food group.

- You believe a good tape job will fix anything.

You **Know** You're a Nurse if ....

- You believe every patient needs TLC: Thorazine, Lorazepam, and Compazine.

- You would like to meet the inventor of the call light in a dark alley one night.

- You believe not all patients are annoying .... Some are unconscious.

- Your sense of humor seems to get more "warped" each year.

- You know the phone numbers of every late night food delivery place in town by heart.

- You can only tell time with a 24-hour clock.

- Almost everything can seem humorous .... Eventually.

- When asked, "What color is the patient's diarrhea?", you show them your shoes.

- Every time you walk, you make a rattling noise because of all the scissors and clamps in your pockets.

- You can tell the pharmacist more about the medicines he is dispensing you than he can.

- You carry "spare" meds in your pocket rather than wait for Pharmacy to deliver.

- You refuse to watch E.R. because it's too much like the real thing and triggers "flash backs."

- You check the caller ID when the phone rings on your day off to see if someone from the hospital is trying to call to ask you to work.

- You've been telling stories in a restaurant and had someone at another table throw up.

- You notice that you use more four letter words now than before you became a nurse.

- very time someone asks you for a pen, you can find at least three at a time on you.

- You can intubate your friends at parties.

- You don't get excited about blood loss ... unless it's your own.

- You live by the motto, "To be right is only half the battle, to convince the physician is more difficult."

- Your bladder can expand to the same size as a Winnebago's water tank.

- You find yourself checking out other customer's arm veins in grocery store waiting lines.

- You can sleep soundly at the hospital cafeteria table during dinner break, sitting up and not be embarrassed when you wake up.

- You avoid unhealthy looking shoppers in the mall for fear that they'll drop and you fear you'll have to do CPR on your day off.

Gynecology Conference ....

During an international gynecology conference, an English doctor and a French doctor were discussing unusual cases they had treated recently.

"Only last week", the Frenchman said, "a woman came to see me with a clitoris like a melon!"

"Don't be absurd", the Brit exclaimed. "It couldn't have been that big — she wouldn't have been able to walk if it were."

"Aaaah, you English, always thinking about size" replied the Frenchman. "I was talking about the flavor!"

Subject: "Doctors"

A little Jewish woman, calling Mount Sinai Hospital, said, "Hello, darling, I'd like to talk with the person who gives the information regarding your patients. I want to know if the patient is getting better or doing like expected, or is getting worse.

The voice on the other end of the line said, "What is the patient's name and room number?"

She said, "Yes darling! She's Sarah Finkel, in Room 302".

He said, "Oh yes Mrs. Finkel is doing very well, in fact, she's had two full meals, her blood pressure is fine, her blood work just came back as normal; she's going to be taken off the heart monitor in a couple of hours and if she continues this improvement, Dr. Cohen is going to send her home Tuesday at twelve o'clock."

The woman said, "Thank God! That's wonderful! Oh! That's fantastic darling! That's wonderful news!"

The man on the phone said, "From your enthusiasm, I take it you must be a close family member or a very close friend!"

She said, "No, I'm Sarah Finkel in room 302! My doctor doesn't tell me shit!"

Be Careful What you Wish for!

A man walking down the beach, sees an old bottle in the sand and begins to play kick-the-bottle to amuse himself. After a while he picks it up, and a pissed off genie emerges.

She says, "Normally I grant 3 wishes, but in your case, you son of a bitch, I am going to grant only one."

He thinks a minute and says, "OK, I want to wake up with 3 women in my bed."

She says, "So be it!" and disappears back into the bottle.

Next morning, he wakes up with Lorena Bobbitt, Tonya Harding, and Hilary Clinton. He has no penis, a broken leg, and no health insurance.

Pay Attention People ! ! ! ! !

Students at the University of Texas Medical School were receiving their first anatomy class with a real dead human body. They are all gathered around the surgery table with the body covered with a white sheet. Then the professor started the class by telling them: "In medicine, it is necessary to have <u>two</u> important qualities as a doctor: The <u>first</u> is that it is necessary that you not be disgusted." The Professor uncovered the body, sunk his finger in the butt of the dead body, withdrew it and sucked it. "Go ahead and do the same thing," he told his students.

The students freaked out, hesitated and subsequently taking turns, sunk their finger in the butt of the dead body and sucked it after withdrawing it.

When everyone finished, the Professor looked at them and told them: "The <u>second</u> important quality is observation. I sunk the middle finger, sucked the INDEX finger. Pay attention people! ! ! "

Hay Doc

A mechanic was removing a cylinder head from the motor of a Harley motorcycle when he spotted a well-known heart surgeon in his shop. The surgeon was there waiting for the service manager to come take a look at his bike. The mechanic shouted across the garage, "Hey Doc, can I ask you a question?"

The surgeon, a bit surprised, walked over to the mechanic working on the motorcycle. The mechanic straightened up, wiped his hands on a rag and asked, "So Doc, look at this engine. I open its heart, take valves out, fix 'em, put 'em back in, and when I finish, it works just like new. So how come I get such a small salary and you get the really big bucks, when you and I are doing basically the same work?

The surgeon paused, smiled and leaned over and whispered to the mechanic......"Try doing it with the engine running!?

Did You Hear this One?

Did you hear about the nurse who died and went straight to hell? It took her two weeks to realize that she wasn't at work anymore!

Top Ten Slogans Currently Being Considered by Viagra :

#10 "Viagra. The quicker dicker upper"

#9 "Here's the beef!"

#8 "Get a piece of the rock"

#7 "You've come a long way, baby"

#6 "Viagra, it plumps when you take 'em"

#5 "Strong enough for a man, but made for a woman"

#4 "Tastes great, more filling"

#3 "Viagra, built ram tough"

#2 "Just do her"

And the number one slogan being considered by Viagra:

#1 "This is your penis. This is your penis on Viagra. Any questions?"

Improving Performance!

With Viagra such a great medical success for increasing men's sexual prowess, Pfizer is bringing forth a whole line of drugs oriented towards improving the performance of men in today's society.... Here are a few of the new ones:

DIRECTRA: A dose of this drug given to men before leaving on car trips caused 72% of them to stop and ask directions when they got lost, compared to a control group of 0.2%.

PROJECTRA: Men given this experimental new drug were far more likely to actually finish a household repair project before starting a new one.

COMPLIMENTRA: In clinical trials, 82% of middle-aged men administered this drug noticed that their wives had a new hairstyle. Currently being tested to see if its effects extend to noticing new clothing.

BUYAGRA: Married and otherwise attached men reported a sudden urge to buy their sweeties expensive jewelry and gifts after taking this drug for only two days. Still to be seen: whether the drug can be continued for a period longer than your favorite store's return limit.

NEGA-VIAGRA: Has the exact opposite effect of Viagra. Currently undergoing clinical trials on sitting U.S. presidents.

NEGA-SPORTAGRA: This drug had the strange effect of making men want to turn off televised sports and actually converse with other family members.

FLATULAGRA: This complex drug converts men's noxious intestinal gases back into food solids. Special bonus: Dosage can be doubled for long car rides.

FLYAGRA: this drug has been showing great promise in treating men with O.F.D. (Open Fly Disorder). Especially useful for men on Viagra.

PRYAGRA: About to fail its clinical trial, this drug gave men in the test group an irresistible urge to dig into the personal affairs of other people. NOTE: Apparent overdose turned three test subjects into "special prosecutors."

LIAGRA: This drug causes men to be less than truthful when being asked about their sexual affairs. Will be available in Regular, Grand Jury, and Presidential Strength versions.

****

Chapter II

LAWYERS . . . . .

GOD should have rested sooner . . . .

Questions! Questions!

- A man walked into a lawyer's office and inquired about the lawyer's rates.

- "$50.00 for three questions, replied the lawyer.

- "Isn't that awfully steep?" asked the man.

- "Yes, " the lawyer replied, "and what was your third question?"

Burrrrrr !! Cold!!

※ It was *so* cold last winter.

※ How cold was it?

※ I saw a lawyer with his hands in his own pockets.

- What do you call 20 lawyers skydiving?   Skeet.

- The Lawyer's Creed: "A man is innocent until proven broke."

? ? ?

- ➤ Did you hear that the Post Office just recalled their latest stamps?
- ➤ They had pictures of lawyers on them....and people couldn't figure out which side to spit on.

- ➤ Why does the law society prohibit sex between lawyers and their clients?
- ➤ To prevent clients from being billed twice for essentially the same service.

- ➤ What's the worst part about seeing 5 lawyers in a Cadillac go over a cliff?
- ➤ A Cadillac seats six!

- ➤ Sadam Housain and a lawyer are buried neck deep in sand, who do you kick in the teeth first?
- ➤ Housain, Business before pleasure.
- ➤ Why don't lawyers go to the beach?
- ➤ Cats keep trying to bury them in the sand.

- ➤ What's the difference between a female attorney and a pit bull?
- ➤ Lipstick.

- ➤ What's black and brown and looks good on an attorney?
- ➤ A Doberman.

- ➤ What do you call 25 attorneys buried up to their chins in cement?
- ➤ Not enough cement.

- ➤ What's the difference between a porcupine and a Porsche with two lawyers riding in it?
- ➤ A porcupine has pricks on the outside.

➤ What do you get when you cross the Godfather with a lawyer?
➤ An offer you can't understand.

➤ What is the definition of a lawyer?
➤ A mouth with a life-support system.

➤ What do you get if you put 100 lawyers in your basement?
➤ A Whine cellar.

➤ Why is an avocado like a lawyer? (both are "avocat" in French)
➤ Both have hearts like stones.

➤ Why are lawyers like nuclear weapons?
➤ If one side has one, the other side has to get one. Once launched during a campaign, they can rarely be recalled. And when they land, they screw up everything forever.

➤ What's the difference between a lawyer and a tick?
➤ A tick drops off you when you die.

➤ What do lawyers and bullfrogs have in common?
➤ Both have a big head that consists mostly of mouth.

➤ What happens when you cross a pig with a lawyer?
➤ Nothing. There are some things a pig won't do.

➤ Out of Towner: Any criminal lawyers in this town?
➤ Local: Yes, But none of them are in jail.

➤ Why is it dangerous for a lawyer to walk onto a construction site when plumbers are working?
➤ Because they might connect the drain line to the wrong sewer.

➤ Why should lawyers wear lots of sunscreen when vacationing at a beach resort?
➤ Because they're used to doing all of their lying indoors.

➤ What's the difference between a lawyer and a prostitute?
➤ A Prostitute will stop screwing you when you're dead.

➤ What do Lawyers and sperm have in common?
➤ They come by the thousands but only one works.

➤ What do you get when you cross a lawyer with a demon from hell?
➤ Another lawyer.

➤ How many lawyers does it take to change a light bulb?
➤ How many can you afford?

➤ What is the difference between a vulture and a lawyer?
➤ The vulture eventually lets go and Vultures don't get Frequent Flyer Miles.

➤ What do you call 5000 dead lawyers at the bottom of the ocean?
➤ A good start!

➤ How can you tell when a lawyer is lying?
➤ His lips are moving.

➤ What's the difference between a dead dog in the road and a dead lawyer in the road?
➤ There are skid marks in front of the dog.

➤ Why won't sharks attack lawyers?
➤ Professional courtesy.

➤ What do you have when a lawyer is buried up to his neck in sand?
➤ Not enough sand.

➤ How do you get a lawyer out of a tree?
➤ Cut the rope.

➤ Do you know how to save a drowning lawyer?
➤ Take your foot off his head.

➤ What's the difference between a lawyer and a bucket of dirt?
➤ The bucket.

➤ What is the definition of a shame (as in "that's a shame")? When a bus load of lawyers goes off a cliff.....
➤ And, what is the definition of a "crying shame"? There was an empty seat!

➤ What can a goose do, a duck can't, and a lawyer should?
➤ Stick his bill up his ass.

➤ Why is it that many lawyers have broken noses?
➤ From chasing parked ambulances.

➤ Where can you find a good lawyer?
➤ In the cemetery.

➤ What's the difference between a lawyer and a gigolo?
➤ A gigolo only screws one person at a time.

➤ What's the difference between a lawyer and a vampire?
➤ A vampire only sucks blood at night.

➤ Why do lawyers wear neckties?
➤ To keep the foreskin from crawling up their chins.

➤ What is the difference between a lawyer and a rooster?
➤ When a rooster wakes up in the morning, it's primal urge is to cluck defiance.

➤ How many law professors does it take to change a light bulb?
➤ Hell, you need 250 just to lobby for the research grant!

➤ If you see a lawyer on a bicycle, why don't you swerve to hit him?

➤ It might be your bicycle.

➤ Why do they bury lawyers under 20 feet of dirt?

➤ Because deep down, they're really good people.

➤ What does a lawyer use for birth control?

➤ His personality.

➤ How many lawyers does it take to change a light bulb?

➤ It only takes one lawyer to change your light bulb to his light bulb.

➤ How many lawyers does it take to change a light bulb?

➤ You won't find a lawyer who can change a light bulb. Now if you're looking for a lawyer to screw a light bulb......

How Many Lawyers Does It Take To Change A Light Bulb?

Whereas the party of the first part, also known as "Lawyer"

and the party of the second part, also known as "Light Bulb", do

hereby and forthwith agree to a transaction wherein the party of

the second part (Light Bulb) shall be removed from the current

position as a result of failure to perform previously agreed upon

duties, i.e., the lighting, elucidation, and otherwise illumination of

the area ranging from the front (north) door, through the entryway, terminating at an area just inside the primary living area, demarcated by the beginning of the carpet, any spillover illumination being at the option of the party of the second part (Light Bulb) and not required by the aforementioned agreement between the parties. The aforementioned removal transaction shall include, but not be limited to, the following steps:

1.   The party of the first part (Lawyer) shall, with or without elevation at his option, by means of a chair, stepstool, ladder or any other means of elevation, grasp the party of the second part (Light Bulb) and rotate the party of the second part (Light Bulb) in a counter-clockwise direction, this point being non-negotiable.

2.   Upon reaching a point where the party of the second part (Light Bulb) becomes separated from the party of the third part ("Receptacle"), the party of the first part (Lawyer) shall have the option of disposing of the party of the second part (Light Bulb) in a manner consistent with all applicable state, local and federal statutes.

3.   Once separation and disposal have been achieved, the party of the first part (Lawyer) shall have the option of beginning installation of the party of the fourth part ("New Light Bulb"). This installation shall occur in a manner consistent with the reverse of the procedures described in step one of this self-same document, being careful to note that the rotation should occur in a clockwise direction, this point also being non-negotiable.

NOTE: The above described steps may be performed, at the option of the party of the first part (Lawyer), by any or all persons authorized by him, the objective being to produce the most possible revenue for the part of the fifth part, also known as "Partnership."

30 Things People Actually said in Court, "Word for Word":

1.   Q: What is your date of birth?
A: July fifteenth.
Q: What year?
A: Every year.

2.   Q: What gear were you in at the moment of the impact?
A: Gucci sweats and Reeboks.

3.
Q: This myasthenia gravis, does it affect your memory at all?
A: Yes.
Q: And in what ways does it affect your memory?
A: I forget.
Q: You forget. Can you give us an example of something that you've forgotten?

4.
Q: How old is your son, the one living with you.
A: Thirty-eight or thirty-five, I can't remember which.
Q: How long has he lived with you?
A: Forty-five years.

5.
Q: What was the first thing your husband said to you when he woke that morning?
A: He said, "Where am I, Cathy?"
Q: And why did that upset you?
A: My name is Susan.

6.
Q: And where was the location of the accident?
A: Approximately milepost 499.
Q: And where is milepost 499?
A: Probably between milepost 498 and 500.

7.
Q: Sir, what is your IQ?
A: Well, I can see pretty well, I think.

8.
Q: Did you blow your horn or anything?
A: After the accident?
Q: Before the accident.
A: Sure, I played for ten years; I eventually went to school for it.

9.
Q: Do you know if your daughter has ever been involved in voodoo or the occult?
A: We both do.

Q: Voodoo?
A: We do.
Q You do?
A: Yes, voodoo.

10.
Q: Trooper, when you stopped the defendant, were your red and blue lights flashing?
A: Yes.
Q: Did the defendant say anything when she got out of her car?
A: Yes, sir.
Q. What did she say?
A: What disco am I at?

11.
Q: Now doctor, isn't it true that when a person dies in his sleep, he doesn't know about it until the next morning?

12.
Q: The youngest son, the twenty-year old, how old is he?

13.
Q: Were you present when your picture was taken?

14.
Q: Was it you or your younger brother who was killed in the war?

15.
Q: Did he kill you?

16.
Q: How far apart were the vehicles at the time of the collision?

17.
Q: You were there until the time you left, is that true?

18
Q: How many times have you committed suicide?

19. Q: Are you qualified to give a urine sample?

20. Q: So the date of conception (of the baby) was August 8th?
A: Yes.
Q: And what were you doing at that time.

21. Q: She had three children, right?
A: Yes.
Q: How many were boys?
A: None.
Q: Were there any girls?

22. Q: You say the stairs went down to the basement?
A: Yes.
Q: And these stairs, did they go up also?

23. Q: Mr. Slatery, you went on a rather elaborate honeymoon, didn't you?
A: I went to Europe, Sir.
Q: And you took your new wife?

24. Q: How was your first marriage terminated?
A: By death.
Q: And by whose death was it terminated?

25. Q: Can you describe the individual?
A: He was bout medium height and had a beard.
Q: Was this a male, or a female.

26. Q: Is your appearance here this morning pursuant to a deposition notice which I sent to your attorney?
     A: No this is how I dress when I go to work.

27. Q: Doctor, how many autopsies have you performed on dead people?
     A: All my autopsies are performed on dead people.

28   Q: All your responses must be oral, OK? What school did you go to?
     A: Oral.

29. Q: Do you recall the time that you examined the body?
     A: The autopsy started around 8:30 p.m.
     Q: And Mr. Dennington was dead at the time?
     A: No, he was sitting on the table wondering why I was doing an autopsy.

30. Q: Doctor, before you performed the autopsy, did you check for a pulse?
     A: No.
     Q: Did you check for blood pressure? .
     A: No.
     Q: Did you check for breathing?
     A: No.
     Q: So, then it is possible that the patient was alive when you began the autopsy?
     A: No.
     Q: How can you be so sure, Doctor?
     A: Because his brain was sitting on my desk in a jar.

Q: But could the patient have still been alive
   nevertheless?

A: It is possible that he could have been alive and
   practicing law somewhere.

Chapter III

MEN, WOMEN and BLONDES

Subject: Dumb Blondes

➢ What does a dumb blonde say when you blow in her ear?
➢ Thanks for the refill.

➢ What's the mating call of the dumb blonde?
➢ Gee, I think I'm drunk.

➢ What can strike a dumb blonde without her knowing it?
➢ A Thought.

➢ Why can't dumb blondes drive?
➢ They don't know what to do once they get in the front seat.

➢ What do a dumb blonde and a bowling ball have in common?
➢ You can pick them up, throw them in the gutter, and they still come back to you.

➢ What does a dumb blonde call brown hair dye?
➢ Artificial Intelligence.

➢ What do you call a brunette between two dumb blondes?
➢ Interpreter.

➢ How does a dumb blonde like her eggs?
➢ Unfertilized.

➢ How do you make a dumb blonde laugh on Monday?
➢ Tell her a joke on Friday.

➢ What's the difference between a dumb blonde and a toothbrush?
➢ You don't let your best friend borrow your toothbrush.

➢ How do dumb blonde brain cells die?
➢ Alone.

➤ How does a dumb blonde lose five pounds?
➤ She takes off her make-up.

➤ Why did it take the dumb blonde three tries to get pregnant?
➤ She blew the first two.

➤ Why don't dumb blondes eat pickles?
➤ They can't get their head in the jar.

➤ Why do dumb blonds drive cars with sun roofs?
➤ More leg room.

➤ What does a dumb blonde call safe sex?
➤ A padded dashboard.

➤ Why did God create dumb blondes?
➤ Because dogs can't bring beer from the fridge.

➤ Why do dumb blondes wear underwear?
➤ To keep their ankles warm.

➤ Why did the dumb blonde have a sore naval?
➤ Her boyfriend was a dumb blonde too!

➤ What's the first thing a dumb blonde does in the morning?
➤ Introduce herself.

➤ What do dumb blondes say after sex?
➤ So, are you guys all on the same team?

➤ How many dumb blondes does it take to screw in a light bulb?
➤ One. She holds it in the socket and waits for the world to revolve around her.

➤ How did the dumb blonde break her leg raking leaves?
➤ She fell out of the tree.

➤ What do you call a dumb blonde with half a brain?
➤ Gifted.

➤ Why do blondes always smile during lightning storms?
➤ They think their picture is being taken.

➤ Why shouldn't blondes have coffee breaks?
➤ It takes too long to retrain them.

➤ What do you call an eternity?
➤ Four blondes at a four-way stop intersection.

➤ What do smart blondes and UFOs have in common?
➤ You always hear about them, but you never see them.

➤ Why does it take longer to build a blonde snowman as opposed to a regular one?
➤ You have to hollow out the head.

➤ How do you get a twinkle in a blonde's eye?
➤ Shine a flashlight in her ear.

➤ Why can't blondes make ice cubes?
➤ They always forget the recipe.

➤ Did you hear about the two blondes that were found frozen to death in their car at a drive-in movie theater?
➤ They went to see "Closed for the Winter."

➤ Why won't they hire blondes as pharmacists?
➤ They keep breaking the prescription bottles in the typewriters.

- ➢ Hear about the blonde that got an AM radio?
- ➢ It took her a month to realize she could play it at night too.

- ➢ What happened to the blonde ice hockey team?
- ➢ They drowned in spring training.

- ➢ What did the blonde say when she saw the sign in front of the YMCA?
- ➢ "Look! They spelled MACYS wrong!"

- ➢ Why did the blonde scale the chain-link fence?
- ➢ To see what was on the other side.

- ➢ Why did the blonde stare at frozen orange juice?
- ➢ Because it said "concentrate".

⌘ A brunette goes to the doctor and as she touches each part of her body with her finger, she says "Doctor it hurts everywhere. My leg hurts, my arm hurts, my back hurts, and even my head hurts!"

The doctor asks, "Were you ever a blonde?"

"Yes, I was," she replies, "why do you ask?"

The doctor answers, "Because your finger is broken!"

⌘ Three blondes were walking through the forest when they came upon a set of tracks.

The first blonde said "Those are dear tracks."

The second blonde said, "No, those are elk tracks."

The third blonde said, "You're both wrong, those are moose tracks.."

The blondes were still arguing when the <u>train</u> hit them!

A young blonde woman is distraught because she fears her husband is having an affair, so she goes to a gun shop and buys a handgun.

The next day she comes home to find her husband in bed with a beautiful redhead. She grabs the gun and holds it to her own head.

The husband jumps out of bed, begging and pleading with her not to shoot herself.

Hysterically, the blonde responds to the husband, "Shut up .... You're next!"

Subject: To All Men Who Send Blonde Jokes

- How many honest, intelligent, caring men in the world does it take to do the dishes?
- Both of them.

- Why did the man cross the road?
- He heard the chicken was a slut.

- Why don't women blink during foreplay?
- They don't have time.

- Why does it take one million sperm to fertilize one egg?
- They won't stop and ask for directions!

- How does a man show that he is planning for the future?
- He buys two cases of beer.

- What is the difference between men and government bonds?
- The bonds mature.

➤ Why are blonde jokes so short?
➤ So men can remember them.

➤ How many men does it take to change a roll of toilet paper?
➤ We don't know; it has never happened.

➤ Why is it difficult to find men who are sensitive, caring, and good looking?
➤ They all already have boyfriends.

➤ What do you call a woman who knows where her husband is every night?
➤ A widow.

➤ When do you care for a man's company?
➤ When he owns it.

➤ How do you get a man to do sit-ups?
➤ Put the remote control between his toes.

➤ What is the one thing that all men at singles bars have in common?
➤ They're married.

➤ Why are married women heavier than single women?
➤ Single women come home, see what's in the fridge and go to bed. Married women come home, see what's in bed and go to the fridge.

✂ Man says to God: "God, why did you make woman so beautiful?"

God says: "So you would love her."

"But God," the man says, "why did you make her so dumb?"

God says: "So she would love you."

Exposure !

➤ A blonde is walking down the street with her blouse open and her right breast hanging out. A policeman approaches her and says, "Ma'am, are you aware that I could cite you for indecent exposure?"

She says, "Why, officer?"

"Because your breast is hanging out."

She looks down and says "OH MY GOD, I left the baby on the bus again!"

River Walk

➤ There's this blonde out for a walk; she comes to a river and sees another blonde on the opposite bank. "Yoo-hoo:" she shouts, "how can I get to the other side?"

The second blonde looks up the river then down the river, then shouts back, "You are on the other side."

Overweight Blonde

➤ A blonde is overweight, so her doctor puts her on a diet. 'I want you to eat regularly for two days, then skip a day and repeat this procedure for two weeks. The next time I see you, you'll have lost at least five pounds."

When the blonde returns, she's lost nearly 20 pounds. "Why, that's amazing!:" the doctor says. "Did you follow my instructions?"

The blonde nods. "I'll tell you though, I thought I was going to drop dead that third day."

"From hunger, you mean?" asked the doctor.

"No, from all that skipping."

Knitting

➤ A highway patrolman pulled alongside a speeding car on the freeway. Glancing at the car, he was astounded to see that the blonde behind the wheel was knitting! Realizing that she was oblivious to his flashing lights and siren, the trooper cranked down his window, turned on his bullhorn and yelled, "PULLOVER!"

"NO," the blonde yelled back, "IT'S A SCARF!"

Blonde on the Sun

➤ A Russian, an American, and a blonde were talking one day. The Russian said, "We were the first in space!"

The American said, "We were the first on the moon!"

The Blonde said, "So what, we're going to be the first on the sun!"

The Russian and the American looked at each other and shook their heads. "You can't land on the sun, you idiot! You'll burn up!" said the Russian.

To which the blonde replied, "We're not stupid, you know, We're going at night!"

Speeding Ticket

➤ A police officer stops a blonde speeding and asks her very nicely if he could see her license. She replied in a huff, "I wish you guys would get your act together. Just yesterday you take away my license and then today you expect me to show it to you!"

The Vacuum

➤ A blonde was playing Trivial Pursuit one night. It was her turn. She rolled the dice and she landed on "Science & Nature." Her question was, "If you are in a vacuum and someone calls your name, can you hear it?" she thought for a time and then asked, "Is it on or off?"

Final Exam

➤ The blonde reported for her university final examination that consists of "yes / no" type questions. She takes her seat in the examination hall, stares at the question paper for five minutes, and then in a fit of inspiration takes her purse out, removes a coin and starts tossing the coin and marking the answer sheet "Yes" for Heads and "No" for Tails.

Within half an hour she is all done, whereas the remainder of the class is sweating it out. During the last few minutes, she is seen desperately throwing the coin, muttering and sweating.

The moderator, alarmed, approaches her and asks what is going on.

"I finished the exam in half an hour, but I'm rechecking my answers."

Subject: She was so Blonde that ....

❖ She sent me a fax with a stamp on it.

❖ She thought a quarterback was a refund.

❖ She tripped over the cordless phone.

❖ At the bottom of the application where it says "sign here,", she put Sagittarius.

❖ If she spoke her mind, she'd be speechless.

❖ When she heard that 90% of all crimes were committed around the home, she moved.

❖ She thinks Taco Bell is a Mexican phone company.

❖ She told me to meet her at the corner of WALK and DON'T WALK.

❖ When she was on the highway going to the airport and saw a sign that said, "Airport Left,", she turned around and went home.

❖ She put lipstick on her forehead because she wanted to make up her mind.

❖ Under education on her job application, she put "Hooked on Phonics."

❖ She studied for a blond test and failed.

❖ She thought Boyz II Men was a daycare center.

❖ It takes her two hours to watch 60 Minutes.

❖   She sold her car so she would have gas money.

❖   She looked into a box of Cheerios and said, "OH, LOOK !! Donut seeds!!"

❖   What do you call five blondes at the bottom of the ocean? An air pocket.

❖   Why do blondes have TGIF on their shirts? "This Goes In Front."

The Blonde Joke to End all Blonde Jokes!

There was a blonde woman who was having financial troubles so she decided to kidnap a child and demand a ransom. She went to a local park, grabbed a little boy, took him behind a tree and wrote this note:

> "I have kidnapped your child. Leave $10,000 in a
> plain brown bag behind the big oak tree in the
> park tomorrow at 7:00 A.M. The Blonde."

She pinned the note inside the little boy's jacket and told him to go straight home. the next morning, she returned to the park to find the $10,000 in a brown bag, behind the big oak tree, just as she had instructed. Inside the bag was the following note.....

> "Here is your money. I cannot believe that one blonde would
> do this to another!"

NOT BLONDE, but . . . . .

When NASA first started sending up astronauts, they quickly discovered that ballpoint pens would not work in zero gravity. To combat the problem, NASA scientists spent a decade and $12 billion to develop a pen that writes in zero gravity, upside down, under water, on almost any surface including glass and at temperatures ranging from below freezing to 300C.

The Russians used a pencil ! !

Chapter IV

KIDS "ARE"
THE DARNDEST THINGS ...

For those **who already have children** past this age, this is hilarious.

For those **who have children this age**, this is not funny.

For those **who have children nearing this age**, this is a warning.

For those **who have not yet had children,** this is a birth control.

The following came from an anonymous mother in Austin, Texas.

THINGS I'VE LEARNED FROM MY CHILDREN ... (HONEST AND NO KIDDING):

- ❖ A king size waterbed holds enough water to fill a 2000 sq. foot house 4 inches deep.

- ❖ If you spray hair spray on dust bunnies and run over them with roller blades, they can ignite.

- ❖ A 3-year old's voice is louder than 200 adults in a crowded restaurant.

- ❖ If you hook a dog leash over a ceiling fan, the motor is not strong enough to rotate a 42 pound boy wearing Batman underwear and a Superman cape. It is strong enough, however, if tied to a paint can, to spread paint on all four walls of a 20 X 20 foot room.

- ❖ You should not throw baseballs up when the ceiling fan is on. When using the ceiling fan as a bat, you have to throw the ball up a few times before you get a hit. A ceiling fan can hit a baseball a long way.

- ❖ The glass in windows (even double pane) doesn't stop a baseball hit by a ceiling fan.

- ❖ When you hear the toilet flush and the words "uh-oh," it's already too late.

- ❖ Brake fluid mixed with Clorox makes smoke, and lots of it.

- ❖ A six-year old can start a fire with a flint rock even though a 36-year old man says they can only do it in the movies. A magnifying glass can start a fire even on an overcast day.

- ❖ Certain LEGOs will pass through the digestive tract of a four-year old.

- ❖ Play Dough and Microwave should never be used in the same sentence.

- ❖ Super glue is forever.

- ❖ No matter how much Jell-O you put in a swimming pool, you still can't walk on water.
- ❖ Pool filters do not like Jell-O.

- ❖ VCR's do not eject PB&J sandwiches even though TV commercials show they do.

- ❖ Garbage bags do not make good parachutes.

- ❖ Marbles in gas tanks make lots of noise when driving.

- ❖ You probably do not want to know what that odor is.

- ❖ Always look in the oven before you turn it on. Plastic toys do not like ovens.

- ❖ The fire department in Austin, TX has a 5-minute response time.

❖ The spin cycle on the washing machine does not make earth worms dizzy.

❖ It will however make cats dizzy.

❖ Cats throw up twice their body weight when dizzy.

Out of the Mouths of Baby's ! ! ! ! ! ! ! ! ! !

A first grade teacher collected old, well-known proverbs. She gave each kid in her class the first half of a proverb, and had them come up with the remainder. These are Great:

☑ As You Shall Make Your Bed, So Shall You . . . **Mess It up.**

☑ Better Be Safe Than . . . **Punch a 5th Grader.**

☑ Strike While The . . . **Bug Is Close.**

☑ It's Always Darkest Before . . . **Daylight Savings Time.**

☑ Never Under Estimate the Power of . . . **Termites.**

☑ You Can Lead a Horse to Water, but . . . **How?**

☑ Don't Bite the Hand That . . . **Looks Dirty.**

☑ No News Is . . . **Impossible.**

☑ A Miss Is As Good As A . . . **Mr.**

☑ You Can't Teach An Old Dog New . . . **Math.**

☑ If You Lie Down With the Dogs, You'll . . . **Stink In the Morning.**

☑ Love All, Trust . . . **Me.**

☑ The Pen Is Mightier Than The ... **Pigs.**

☑ An Idle Mind Is ... **The Best Way to Relax.**

☑ Where There's Smoke, There's ... **Pollution.**

☑ Happy the Bride Who ... **Gets All The Presents!**

☑ A Penny Saved Is ... **Not Much.**

☑ Two's Company, Three's ... **The Musketeers.**

☑ Don't Put Off to Tomorrow What ... **You Put On To Go To Bed.**

☑ Laugh and the Whole World Laughs With You, Cry and . **You Have to Blow Your Nose.**

☑ None Are So Blind As ... **Helen Keller.**

☑ Children should be Seen and Not ... **Spanked or Grounded.**

☑ If At First You don't Succeed ... **Get New Batteries.**

☑ You Get Out of Something What You ... **See Pictured On the Box.**

☑ When the Blind Leadeth the Blind ... **Get Out of The Way.**

☑ There Is No Fool Like ... **Aunt Eddie.**

CHILDREN'S GEMS:

It was Palm Sunday and, because of a sore throat, little 5-year old Johnny stayed home from church with a sitter. When the family returned home, they were carrying several palm branches. The boy asked what they were for, "People held them over Jesus' head as he walked by," his oldest brother explained. "Wouldn't you know it,", the boy fumed. "The one Sunday I don't go, He showed up!"

****

One Easter Sunday morning as the minister was preaching the children's sermon, he reached into his bag of props and pulled out an egg. He pointed at the egg and asked the children, "What's in here?"

"I know" a little boy exclaimed. "Pantyhose!"

****

When my grandson, Billy, and I entered our vacation cabin, we kept the lights off until we were inside to keep from attracting pesky insects. Still a few fireflies followed us in. Noticing them before I did, Billy whispered "It's no use Grandpa," Billy said. "The mosquitoes are coming after us with flashlights."

****

The prospective father-in-law asked, "Young man, can you support a family?" The surprised groom-to-be replied, "Well, no I was just planning to support your daughter. The rest of you will have to fend for yourselves."

****

Little Johnny asked his grandpa how old he was. Grandpa answered, "39 and holding."

Johnny thought for a moment, and then said, "And how old would you be if you let go?"

****

As Mom was preparing pancakes for her sons, Johnny, 5 and Alex, 3, the boys began to argue over who would get the first pancake. The Mom saw the opportunity to teach a moral lesson. She said, "If Jesus were sitting here, He would say "Let my brother have the first pancake, I can wait."

Johnny turned to his younger brother and said, "Okay, Alex, you be Jesus."

****

A little boy in church for the first time watched as the ushers passed the offering plates. When they came near his pew, the boy said loudly, "don't pay for me Daddy, I'm under 5."

****

The Sunday School teacher asked, "Now Johnny, tell me, do you say prayers before eating?" "No Sir," he replied.

"We don't have to, my Mom is a good cook."

****

"Oh, I sure am happy to see you." The little boy said to his grandmother on his mother's side. "Now maybe Daddy will do the trick he has been promising us."

The Grandmother was curious. "What trick is that?"
"I heard him tell Mommy", "the little boy answered, "That he would climb the walls if you came to visit."

After putting her children to bed, a mother changed into old slacks and droopy blouse and proceeded to wash her hair. As she heard the children getting more and more rambunctious, her patience grew thin. At last she threw a towel around her head and stormed into their room, putting them back in bed with stern warnings. As she left the room, she heard her 3-year old say with a trembling voice, "Who was THAT?!"

****

A mother was telling her little girl what her own childhood was like: "We used to skate outside on a pond. I had a swing made from a tire, it hung from a tree in our front yard. We rode our pony. We picked wild raspberries in the woods."

The little girl was wide-eyed, taking this in. At last she said, "I sure wish I'd gotten to know you sooner.

****

My grandson was visiting one day when he asked, "Grandma, do you know how you and God are alike?" I mentally polished my halo while I asked, "No how are we alike?"

You're both old," he replied.

****

I didn't know if my granddaughter had learned her colors yet, so I decided to test her. I would point out something and ask what color it was. She would tell me, and always she was correct. But it was fun for me, so I continued.
At last she headed for the door, saying sagely, "Grandma, I think you should try to figure out some of these yourself!!"

****

A Sunday School Class was studying The Ten commandments. They were ready to discuss the last one. The teacher asked if anyone could tell her what it was.

Susie raised her hand, stood tall, and quoted," Thou shalt not take the covers off thy neighbor's wife."

The Wisdom of Children

WHAT PROMISES DO A MAN AND A WOMAN MAKE WHEN THEY GET MARRIED?"A man and a woman promise to go through sickness and illness and diseases together."

Marion, age 10

WHAT WOULD YOU SUGGEST TO MAKE A MARRIAGE WORK? "Tell your wife that she looks pretty even if she looks like a truck!"

Ricky, age 7

"If you want to last with your man, you should wear a lot of sexy clothes . . . . Especially underwear that is red and maybe has a few diamonds on it."

Lori, age 8

ABOUT GETTING MARRIED FOR A SECOND TIME......"Most men are brainless, so you might have to try more than one to find a live one."

Angie L., age 10

HOW WOULD THE WORLD BE DIFFERENT IF PEOPLE DIDN'T GET MARRIED?"There sure would be a lot of kids to explain, wouldn't there?"

Kelvin, age 8

WHAT WOULD YOU DO ON A FIRST DATE?"I'd run home and play dead. The next day I would call all the newspapers and make sure they wrote about me in all the dead columns."

Craig, Age 9

WHEN IS IT OKAY TO KISS SOMEONE?"When they're rich!"

Pam, age 7

"The law says you have to be eighteen, so I wouldn't want to mess with that."

Curt, age 7

"The rule goes like this: If you kiss someone, then you should marry them and have kids with them . . . . It's the right thing to do."

Howard, age 8

IS IT BETTER TO BE SINGLE OR MARRIED?"I don't know which is better, but I'll tell you one thing; I'm never going to have sex with my wife. I don't want to be all grossed out!:"

Theodore, age 8

"It's better for girls to be single but not for boys. Boys need some-body to clean up after them!:"

Anita, age 9

"Single is better . . . for the simple reason that I wouldn't want to change no diapers . . . Of course, if I did get married, I'd figure some-thing out. I'd just phone my mother and have her come over for some coffee and diaper-changing."

Kirsten, age 10

WHAT ADVICE DO YOU HAVE FOR A YOUNG COUPLE ABOUT TO BE MARRIED?"The first thing I'd say to them is, 'Listen up, young'uns. . . I got something to say to you. Why in the heck do you wan' a get married, anyway?'"

Craig, age 9

HOW DOES A PERSON DECIDE WHO TO MARRY?"You flip a nickel, and heads means you stay with him and tails means you try the next one."

Kally, age 9

"You got to find somebody who likes the same stuff. Like if you like sports, she should like it that you like sports, and she should keep the chips and dip coming."

Allan, age 10

"No person really decides before they grow up who they're going to marry. God decides it all way before and you got to find out later who you're stuck with."

Kirsten, age 10

WHAT'S THE PROPER AGE TO GET MARRIED?"Twenty-three is the best age because you know the person FOREVER by then!"

Cam, age 10

"No age is good to get married at . . . . You got to be a fool to get married!"

Freddie, age 6

HOW CAN A STRANGER TELL IF TWO PEOPLE ARE MARRIED?"Married people usually look happy to talk to other people."

Eddie, age 6

"You might have to guess based on whether they seem to be yelling at the same kids."

Derrick, age 8

WHAT DO YOU THINK YOUR MOM AND DAD HAVE IN COMMON?"Both don't want no more kids."

Lori, age 8

WHAT DO MOST PEOPLE DO ON A DATE?"Dates are for having fun and people should use them to get to know each other. Even boys have something to say if you listen long enough."

Lynette, age 8

"On the first date, they just tell each other lies, and that usually gets them interested enough to go for a second date."

Martin, age 10

KIDS' ADVICE TO OTHER KIDS ...

* Never trust a dog to watch your food. Patrick, age 10

* When your dad is mad and asks you, "Do I look stupid?", don't answer him, and never tell your mom her diet's not working. Michael, 14

* Stay away from prunes. Randy, 9

* Don't squat with your spurs on. Noronha, 13

* Don't pull dad's finger when he tells you to. Emily, 10

* When your mom is mad at your dad, don't let her brush your hair. Taylia, 11

* Never allow your 3-year old brother in the same room as your school assignment. Traci, 14

* Don't sneeze in front of mum when you're eating crackers. Mitchell, 12

* Puppies still have bad breath even after eating a Tic-Tac. Andrew, 9

* Never hold a dust buster and a cat at the same time. Kyoyo, 9

* You can't hide a piece of broccoli in a glass of milk. Armir, 9

* If you want a kitten, start out by asking for a horse. Naomi, 15

* Felt markers are not good to use as lipstick. Lauren, 9

* Don't pick on your sister when she's holding a baseball bat. Joel, 10

* When you get a bad grade in school, show it to your mom when she's on the phone. Alyesha, 13

* Don't wear polka-dot underwear under white shorts.

  Kellie, 11

Some Things to Think About ......

1) Parenthood ... if it was going to be easy, it never would have started with something like labor!

2) Shouting to make your children obey is like using the horn to steer your car, and you get about the same results.

3) To be in your children's memories tomorrow, you have to be in their lives today.

4) The smartest advise on raising children is to enjoy them while they are on your side.

5) Avenge yourself. Live long enough to be a problem to your children.

6) The best way to keep kids at home is to make home a pleasant atmosphere ... and to let the air out of the tires!

7) The right temperature in a home is maintained by warm hearts, not by hot heads.

8) Parents: People who bear infants, bore teenagers, and board newlyweds.

9) The joy of parenthood: What a parent experiences when all the children are finally in bed.

10) Life's golden age is when the kids are too old to need baby-sitters and too young to borrow the family car.

11) Any child can tell you that the sole purpose of a middle name is so he can tell when he's really in trouble.

12) Grandparents are similar to a piece of string . . . . handy to have around and easily wrapped around the fingers of grandchildren.

13) A child outgrows your lap, but never outgrows your heart.

14) You have two ears and one mouth . . . so you could listen twice as much as you talk.

15) There are three ways to get something done; Do it your-self, hire someone to do it, or forbid your children to do it.

16) Adolescence is the age when children try to bring up their parents.

17) You know the only people in the world who are always sure about the proper way to raise children? Those who've never had any.

18) Cleaning your house while your kids are at home is like trying to shovel the driveway during a snowstorm.

19) Oh to be only half as wonderful as my child thought I was when he was small, and half as stupid as my teenager now thinks I am.

20) There are only two things a child will share willingly: communicable diseases and his mother's age.

21) Money isn't everything. But it sure keeps the kids in touch.

22) Adolescence is the age at which children stop asking questions because they know all the answers.

23) An alarm clock is a device for awakening people who don't have small children.

24) How do you cope when the apple of your eye becomes a bone in your throat?

25) No wonder kids are confused today. Half the adults tell them to find themselves; the other half tell them to get lost.

26) The persons hardest to convince they're at the retirement age are the children at bedtime.

27) Kids really brighten a household; they never turn off any lights!

Chapter V

GOD, CHURCH, AND REAPING WHAT WE SOW . . .

Slow Dance

Have you ever watched kids on a merry-go-round,
or listened to rain slapping the ground?

Ever followed a butterfly's erratic flight,
or gazed at the sun into the fading night?

You better slow down, don't dance so fast,
time is short, the music won't last.

Do you run through each day on the fly,
when you ask "How are you", do you hear the reply?

When the day is done, do you lie in your bed,
with the next hundred chores running through your head?

You better slow down, don't dance so fast,
Time is short, the music won't last.

Ever told your child, we'll do it tomorrow,
And in your haste, not seen his sorrow?

Ever lost touch, let a good friendship die,
'cause you never had time to call and say "Hi".

You better slow down, don't dance so fast,
time is short, the music won't last.

When you run so fast to get somewhere,
You miss half the fun of getting there.

When you worry and hurry through your day,
It is like and unopened gift thrown away.

Life is not a race, so take it slower,
hear the music before the song is over!

Understanding God's Plan:

Understand that God anoints you for trouble. Be sure you are a Christian. Put on the armor of God before going to work.

Don't expect to be appreciated. Your only expectation should be to get a paycheck. Don't come to work to have personal relationships. Don't allow what you do to affect who you are.

Do your job well, but remember your mission. God put you there to be a light.

Seek opportunities to change the atmosphere without commenting on the problems. You have a God to talk to. You're on an assignment. In quietness and competence shall be our strength.

Don't let your environment get inside of you. You should influence it, not let it influence you. Stop going to work to be fed – you didn't come to receive, you came to give.

Increase your capacity to work with different personalities. God will often bless you through people you don't even like!

Remember where you are does not define where you are going. This will deliver you from frustration. God has a plan for your life. Keep your eye on the prize. When Peter did this, he was able to walk in what other people sank in!

Get the optimum results with minimal confusion. Be effective without making the environment worse.

Don't be associated with one group or clique. Labels limit your usefulness. God wants you to work with everybody but be labeled by nobody. Use all your gifts.

Always keep your song near you. Keep a consecrated place in your soul. Hold on to your praise.

When I Whine....

Today, upon a bus,
I saw a girl with golden hair,
and wished I was as fair.
When suddenly she rose to leave,
I saw her hobble down the aisle.
She had one leg and wore a crutch,
but as she passed, she passed a smile.

Oh, god, forgive me when I whine.
I have 2 legs, the world is mine.

I stopped to buy some candy.
The lad who sold it had such charm.
I talked with him, he seemed so glad.
If I were late, it'd do no harm.
And as I left, he said to me,
"I thank you, you've been so kind.
It's nice to talk with folks like you.
You see," he said, "I'm blind."

Oh, god, forgive me when I whine.
I have 2 eyes, the world is mine.

Later while walking down the street,
I saw a child with eyes of blue.
He stood and watched the others play.
He did not know what to do.
I stopped a moment and then I said,
"Why don't you join the others, dear?"
He looked ahead without a word.
And then I knew, he couldn't hear.

Oh, God forgive me when I whine.
I have 2 ears, the world is mine.

With feet to take me where I'd go.
With eyes to see the sunset's glow.
With ears to hear what I'd know.
Oh, God forgive me when I whine.
I've been blessed indeed, the world is mine.

What In the World is Happening with our Kids Today?

Let's see ...

I think it started when Madelyn Murray O'Hair complained that she didn't want any PRAYER in our schools, and WE said "O.K."

Then someone said, "You had better not read the Bible in school, the Bible that says,
Thou shalt not kill, thou shalt not steal, AND Love your neighbor as yourself."
And WE said "O.K."

Remember Dr. Benjamin Spock, who said we shouldn't spank our children when they misbehave, because their little personalities would be warped and we might damage their self-esteem?
And WE said "O.K."

Better not discipline our children when they misbehave. And our Administrators said, "Whoa, no one in this school better touch a student when they misbehave because we don't want any bad publicity, and we surely don't want to be sued."
And WE said "O.K."

Then someone said, "Let's let our daughters have abortion if they want, we won't even have to tell their parents."
And WE said "O.K."

Then someone else said, "Let's give our sons and daughters all the condoms they want, they can have all the "FUN" they desire, and we won't have to tell their parents."
And WE said "O.K."

And then some of our top officials said that it doesn't matter what we do in private as long as we do our jobs. And we said, "As long as I have a job and the economy is good, it doesn't matter to me what anyone does in private, it's nobody's business."
In short, WE said "O.K."

So now we're asking ourselves why our children have no conscience?
Why they don't know right from wrong?
Why it doesn't bother them to kill?

Probably, if we think about it long and hard enough,

WE can figure it out.
I think it has a great deal to do with

"WHAT WE REAP IS WHAT WE SOW."

Whoa! What a concept!

Be Thankful!

I am God. Today I will be handling all of your problems.
Please remember that I do not need your help.

If life happens to deliver a situation to you that you cannot
handle, do not attempt to resolve it.
Kindly put it in the SFGTD (something for God to do) Box.
All situations will be resolved, but in MY time, NOT yours.

Once the matter is placed into the box, do not hold onto
it by worrying about it.
Instead, focus on all the wonderful things that are present
in your life now.

If you find yourself stuck in traffic, don't despair.
There are people in this world for whom driving is an un-
heard of privilege.

Should you have a bad day at work, think of the man who
has been out of work for years.

Should you despair over a relationship gone bad,
think of the person who has never known what it's like to
love and be loved in return.

Should you grieve the passing of another weekend,

think of the woman in dire straits, working twelve hours a day, seven days a week to feed her children.

Should your car break down, leaving you miles away from assistance,
think of the paraplegic who would love the opportunity to take that walk.

Should you notice a new gray hair in the mirror,
think of the cancer patient in chemo who wishes he/she had hair to examine.

Should you find yourself at a loss and pondering what life is all about,
asking what is my purpose?   Be thankful.
There are those who didn't live long enough to get the opportunity.

Should you find yourself the victim of other people's bitterness,
ignorance, smallness or insecurities,
remember, things could be worse.
You could be one of them!

The Right Hymn for the Right Person.....

The Dentist's Hymn . . . . "Crown Him with Many Crowns"

The Weatherman's Hymn . . . . "There Shall Be Showers of Blessings"

The Contractor's Hymn   . . . . "The Church's One Foundation"

The Tailor's Hymn . . . . "Holy, Holy, Holy"

The Golfer's Hymn . . . . "There's a Green Hill Far Away"

The Politician's Hymn . . . . "Standing on the Promises"

The Optometrist's Hymn . . . . "Open My Eyes That I Might See"

The IRS Agent's Hymn . . . . "I Surrender All"

The Gossip's Hymn . . . . "Pass It On"

The Electrician's Hymn . . . . "Send The Light"

The Shopper's Hymn . . . . "Sweet By and By"

The Realtor's Hymn . . . . "I've Got A Mansion, Just Over the Hilltop"

The Massage Therapists Hymn . . . . . . "He Touched Me"

The Doctor's Hymn . . . . "The Great Physician"

For Those Who Speed On The Highway – A Few Hymns:

45 mph . . . . "God Will Take Care of You"

55 mph . . . . "Guide Me, O Thou Great Jehovah"

65 mph . . . . "Nearer My God To Thee"

75 mph . . . . "Nearer Still Nearer"

85 mph . . . . "This World Is Not My Home"

95 mph. . . . . "Lord, I'm Coming Home"

And over 100 mph. . . . . "Precious Memories"

PRAYERS:

Give me a sense of humor, Lord,

Give me the grace to see a joke,

To get some humor out of life,

And pass it on to other folk.
Amen.

Every single evening
As I'm lying here in bed
This tiny little prayer
Keeps running through my head.

God bless all my family
Wherever they may be,
Keep them warm and safe from harm
For they're so close to me.

And God, there is one more thing
I wish that you could do.
Hope you don't mind me asking,
Bless my computer too.

Now I know that it's not normal
To bless a mother board,
But listen just a second
While I explain to you 'My Lord'.

You see, that little metal box
Holds more than odds and ends

Inside those small compartments
Rest so many of my FRIENDS.

I know so much about them
By the kindness that they give
And this little scrap of metal
Takes me in to where they live.

By faith is how I know them
Much the same as you
We share in what life brings us
And from that our friendship grew.

Ten Ways To Know You're In The Wrong Church !

1) The church bus has gun racks.

2) The church staff consists of Senior Pastor, Associate Pastor, and Socio-pastor.

3) They use the "Dr. Seuss Version" of the Bible.

4) There's an ATM in the lobby.

5) The choir wears leather robes.

6) Worship services are B.Y.O.S. ("Bring Your Own Snake")

7) There's no cover charge, but communion is a two-drink minimum.

8) They have Karaoke Worship Time.

9) Ushers ask, "Smoking or non-smoking?"

10) The only song the organist knows is "In-A-Gadda-Da-Vida."

P. U. S. H. !

The Lord responded compassionately, "My friend, when I asked you to serve Me and you accepted I told you that your task was to push against the rock with all of your strength, which you have done.

Never once did I mention to you that I expected you to move it. Your task was to push. And now you come to Me with your strength spent, thinking that you have failed. But, is that really so?

Look at yourself. Your arms are strong and muscled, back sinewy and brown, your hands are callused from constant pressure, your legs have become massive and hard.

Through opposition, you have grown much, and your abilities now surpass that which you used to have. Yet you haven't moved the rock. But your calling was to be obedient and to push and to exercise your faith and trust in My wisdom. This you have done.

Now I, My friend, will move the rock."

At times, when we hear a word from God, we tend to use our own intellect to decipher what He wants, when actually what God wants is just a simple obedience and faith in Him.

By all means, exercise the faith that moves mountain, but know that it is still God who moves mountains.

When everything seems to go wrong ... just P. U. S. H. !

When the job gets you down ... just P. U. S. H.

When people don't react the way you think they should ... just P. U. S. H. !

When your money looks "gone" and the bills are due ... just P. U. S. H.!

When people just don't understand you ... just P. U. S. H.!

P = Pray
U = Until
S = Something
H = Happens !

The B . I. B. L. E.

A father was approached by his small son, who told him proudly, "I know what the Bible means!

His father smiled and replied ... "What do you mean, you 'know' what the Bible means?"

The son replied, "I do know!"

"Okay," said his father, "So, son, what does the Bible mean?"

"That's easy, Daddy ....."

It stands for "**B**asic **I**nstructions **B**efore **L**eaving **E**arth."

Leave it to a child to figure it out !

****

Friends are angels
who lift us up
when our wings
have trouble remembering
how to fly.

****

YOU ARE BLESSED.

If you own just one Bible, you are abundantly blessed. One third of the world does not have access to even one.

If you woke up this morning with more health than illness, you are more blessed than the million who will not survive the week.

If you have never experienced the danger of battle, the loneliness of imprisonment, the agony of torture or the pangs of starvation, you are ahead of 500 million people around the world.

If you attend a church meeting without fear of harassment, arrest or torture of death, you are more blessed than almost three billion people in the world.

If you have food in your refrigerator, clothes on your back, a roof over your head and a place to sleep, you are richer than 75% of this world.

If you have money in the bank, in your wallet, and spare change in a dish someplace, you are among the top 8% of the world's wealthy.

If your parents are still married and alive, you are very rare, even in the United States.

If you hold up your head with a smile on your face and are truly thankful, you are blessed because the majority can, but most do not.

If you can hold someone's hand, hug them or even touch them on the shoulder, you are blessed because you can offer God's healing touch.

If you prayed yesterday and today, you are in the minority because you believe in God's willingness to hear and answer prayer.

If you believe in Jesus as the Son of God, you are part of a very small minority in the world.

If you can read this message, you are more blessed than over two billion people in the world that cannot read anything at all.

Just in Case you Needed to be Reminded Today:

Right now, -   somebody is very proud of you.

- somebody is thinking of you.

- somebody is caring about you.

- somebody misses you.

- somebody wants to talk to you.

- somebody wants to be with you.

- somebody hopes you aren't in trouble.

- somebody is thankful for the support you have provided.

- somebody wants to hold your hand.

- somebody hopes everything turns out all right.

- somebody wants you to be happy.

- somebody wants you to find him / her.

- somebody is celebrating your successes.

- somebody wants to give you a gift.

- somebody thinks that you are a gift.

- somebody hopes you're not too cold, or too hot.

- somebody wants to hug you.

- somebody loves you.

- somebody wishes you would lavish them with small things.

- somebody admires your strength.

- somebody is thinking of you and smiling.

- somebody wants to be your shoulder to cry on.

- somebody wants to go out with you and have a lot of fun.

- somebody thinks the world of you.

- somebody wants to protect you.

- somebody would do anything for you.

- somebody wants to be forgiven.

- somebody is grateful for your forgiveness.

- somebody wants to laugh with you about old times.

- somebody remembers you and wishes that you were there.

- somebody is praising God for you.

- somebody needs to know that your love is unconditional.

- somebody values your advice.

- somebody wants to tell you how much they care.

- somebody wants to stay up watching old movies with you.

- somebody wants to share their dreams with you.

- somebody wants to hold you in their arms.

- somebody wants you to hold them in your arms.

- somebody treasures your spirit.

- somebody wishes they could stop time because of you.

- somebody praises god for your friendship and love.

- somebody can't wait to see you.

- somebody wishes that things didn't have to change.

- somebody loves you for who you are.

- somebody loves the way you make them feel.

- somebody is hoping they can grow old with you.

- somebody hears a song that reminds them of you.

- somebody wants you to know they are there for you.

- somebody is glad that you're his/her friend.

- somebody wants to be your friend.

- somebody stayed up all night thinking about you.

- somebody is alive because of you.

- somebody is very remorseful after losing your friendship.

- somebody is wishing that you noticed him/her.

- somebody wants to get to know you better.

- somebody believes that you are his/her soul mate.

- somebody wants to be near you.

- somebody misses your advice/guidance.

- somebody has faith in you.

- somebody trusts you.

- somebody needs you to send them a letter or post-card.

- somebody needs your support.

- somebody needs you to have faith in them.

- somebody will cry when they read this.

- somebody needs you to let them be your friend.

- SOMEBODY NEEDS YOU TO SHARE THIS WITH THEM!

A Good Reminder for those 'BLUE' Days ...

The only survivor of a shipwreck was washed up on a small, uninhabited island. He prayed feverishly for God to rescue him, and every day he scanned the horizon for help, but none seemed forthcoming. Exhausted, he eventually managed to build a little hut out of driftwood to protect him from the elements, and to store his few possessions. But then one day, after scavenging for food, he arrived home to find his little hut in flames, the smoke rolling up to the sky.

The worst had happened; everything was lost. He was stunned with grief and anger. "God, how could you do this to me!" he cried.

Early the next day, however, he was awakened by the sound of a ship that was approaching the island. It had come to rescue him.

"How did you know I was here?" asked the weary man of his rescuers.

"We saw your smoke signal," they replied.

It is easy to get discouraged when things are going bad. But we shouldn't lose heart, because God is at work in our lives, even in the midst of pain and suffering. Remember, next time your little hut is burning to the ground - - it just may be a smoke signal that summons the grace of God.

For all the negative things we have to say to ourselves, God has a positive answer for it:

You say: "It's impossible"
God says: *"All things are possible"* (Luke 18:27)

You say: "I'm too tired"
God says: *"I will give you rest"* (Matthew 11:28-30)

You say: "Nobody really loves me"
God says: *"I love you"* (John 3:16 & John 13:34)

You say: "I can't go on"
God says: *"My grace is sufficient"* (II Corinthians 12:9 & Psalm 91:15)

You say: "I can't figure things out"
God says: *"I will direct your steps"* (Proverbs 3:5-6)

You say: "I can't do it"
God says: *"You can do all things"* (Philippians 4:13)

You say: "It's not worth it"
God says: *"It will be worth it"* (Romans 8:28)

You say: "I can't forgive myself"
God says: *"I FORGIVE YOU"* (I John 1:9 & Romans 8:1)

You say: "I can't manage"
God says: *"I will supply all your needs"* (Philippians 4:19)

You say: "I'm afraid"
God says: *"I have not given you a spirit of fear"* (II timothy 1:7)

You say: "I'm always worried and frustrated"
God says: *"Cast all your cares on ME"* (I Peter 5:7)

You say: "I don't have enough faith"
God says: *"I've given everyone a measure of faith"* (Romans 12:3)

You say: "I'm not smart enough"
God says: *"I give you wisdom"* (I Corinthians 1:30)

You say: "I feel all alone"
God says: *"I will never leave you or forsake you"* (Hebrews
              13:5)

With GOD, all things are possible. HE makes good out of bad, when WE let HIM.

Thank God for Church Ladies with Typewriters.

These sentences actually appeared in church bulletins or were announced in church services:

1) I, Bertha Belch, a missionary from Africa, will be speaking tonight at Calvary Methodist. Come hear Bertha Belch all the way from Africa.

2) Announcement in a church bulletin for a national PRAYER & FASTING Conference. "The cost for attending the Fasting & Prayer Conference includes meals."

3) The sermon this morning "Jesus Walks on the Water". Sermon tonight "Searching for Jesus".

4) Our youth basketball team is back in action Wednesday at 8:00 p.m. in the recreation hall. Come out and watch us kill Christ the King.

5) Ladies don't forget the rummage sale. It's a chance to get rid of those things not worth keeping around the house. Don't forget your husbands.

6) The peacemaking meeting scheduled for today has been cancelled due to a conflict.

7) Remember in prayer the many who are sick of our community. Smile at someone who is hard to love. Say "Hell" to someone who doesn't care much about you.

8) Don't let worry kill you off — let the Church help.

9) Miss Charlene Mason sang "I will Not Pass This Way Again," giving obvious pleasure to the congregation.

10) For those of you who have children and don't know it, we have a nursery downstairs.

11) Next Thursday, there will be tryouts for the choir. They need all the help they can get.

12) Barbara remains in the hospital and needs blood donors for more transfusions. She is also having trouble sleeping and requests tapes of Pastor Jack's sermons.

13) The Rector will preach his farewell message after which the choir will sing "Break Forth Into Joy."

14) Irving Benson and Jessie Carter were married on October 24th in the church. So ends a friendship that began in their school days.

15) A bean supper will be held on Tuesday evening in the church hall. Music will follow.

16) At the evening service tonight, the sermon topic will be "What is Hell?" Come early and listen to our choir practice.

17) Eight new choir robes are currently needed due to the addition of several new members and to the deterioration of some older ones.

18) Scouts are saving aluminum cans, bottles, and other items to be recycled. Proceeds will be used to cripple children.

19) Please place your donation in the envelope along with the deceased person you want remembered.

20) Attend and you will hear an excellent speaker and heave a health lunch.

21) The church will host an evening of fine dining, superb entertainment, and gracious hostility.

22) Potluck supper Sunday at 5:00 PM – prayer and medication to follow.

23) The ladies of the Church have cast off clothing of every kind. They may be seen in the basement on Friday afternoon.

24) This evening at 7:00 PM there will be a hymn sing in the park across from the Church. Bring a blanket and come prepared to sin.

25) Ladies Bible Study will be held Thursday morning at 10:00 AM. All ladies are invited to lunch in the Fellowship Hall after the B.S is done.

26) The pastor would appreciate it if the ladies of the congregation would lend him their electric girdles for the pancake breakfast next Sunday.

27) Low Self Esteem Support Group will meet Thursday at 7:00 PM. Please use the back door.

28) The eighth-graders will be presenting Shakespeare's Hamlet in the church basement Friday at 7:00 PM. The congregation is invited to attend this tragedy.

29) Weight Watchers will meet at 7:00 PM at the First Presbyterian Church. Please use large double door at the side entrance.

30) The Associate Minister unveiled the church's new tithing campaign slogan last Sunday: "I Upped My Pledge – Up Yours."

"Deck of Cards"

A young soldier was in his bunkhouse all alone one Sunday morning over in Afghanistan. It was quiet that day, the guns and the mortars, and land mines, for some reason hadn't made a noise. The young soldier knew it was Sunday, the holiest day of the week. As he was sitting there, he got out an old deck of cards and laid them out across his bunk.

Just then an Army sergeant came in and said, "Why aren't you with the rest of the platoon?"

The soldier replied, "I thought I would stay behind and spend some time with the Lord."

The sergeant said "Looks like you're going to play cards."

The soldier said, "No sir, you see, since we are not allowed to have Bibles or other spiritual books in this country, I've decided to talk to the Lord by studying this deck of cards."

The Sergeant asked in disbelief, "How will you do that?"

"You see the Ace, Sergeant, it reminds that there is only one God.

The Two represents the two parts of the Bible, Old and New Testaments.

The Three represents the Father, the Son, and the Holy Ghost.

The Four stands for the Four Apostles: Matthew, Mark, Luke, and John.

The Five is for the five virgins that were ten but only five of them were glorified.

The Six is for the six days it took God to create the Heavens and Earth.

The Seven is for the day God rested after working the six days.

The Eight is for the family of Noah and his wife, their three sons and their wives,
in which God saved the eight people from the flood that destroyed the earth for the first time.

The Nine is for the lepers that Jesus cleansed of leprosy. He cleansed ten but nine never thanked Him.

The Ten represents the Ten Commandments that God handed down to Moses on tablets made of stone.

The Jack is a reminder of Satan. One of God's first angels, but he got kicked out of heaven for his sly and wicked ways and is now the joker of eternal hell.

The queen stands for the Virgin Mary.

The King stands for Jesus, for he is the KING OF ALL KINGS.

When I count the dots on all the cards, I come up with 365 total, one for every day of the year.

There are a total of 52 cards in a deck, each is a week, 52 weeks in a year.

The four suits represents the four seasons: Spring, Summer, Fall, and Winter.

Each suit has thirteen cards, there are exactly thirteen weeks in a quarter.

So when I want to talk to God and thank Him, I just pull out this old deck of cards and they remind me of all that I have to be thankful for."

The sergeant just stood there and after a minute, with tears in his eyes and pain in his heart, he said, "*Soldier, can I borrow that deck of cards?*"

Chapter VI

OUR
BELOVED
ANIMALS and PETS

What is a Cat?

1) Cats do what they want.
2) They rarely listen to you.
3) They're totally unpredictable.
4) They whine when they are not happy.
5) When you want to play, they want to be alone.
6) When you want to be alone, they want to play.
7) They expect you to cater to their every whim.
8) They're moody.
9) They leave hair everywhere.
10) They drive you nuts and cost an arm and a leg.

Conclusion: They're tiny women in little fur coats!

What is a Dog?

1) Dogs lie around all day, sprawled on the most comfortable piece of furniture in the house.
2) They can hear a package of food opening half a black away, but don't hear you when you're in the same room.
3) They can look dumb and lovable all at the same time.
4) They growl when they are not happy.
5) When you want to play, they want to play.
6) When you want to be alone, they want to play.
7) They are great at begging.
8) They will love you forever if you rub their tummies.
9) They leave their toys everywhere.
10) They do disgusting things with their mouths and then try to give you a kiss.

Conclusion: They're tiny men in little fur coats.

How To Medicate Your Cat Or Dog.....

Cat:

1) Pick cat up and cradle it in the crook of your left arm as if holding a baby. Position right forefinger and thumb on either side of cat's mouth and gently apply pressure to cheeks while holding pill in right hand. As cat opens mouth, pop pill into mouth. Allow cat to close mouth and swallow.

2) Retrieve pill from floor and cat from behind sofa. Cradle cat in left arm and repeat process.

3) Retrieve cat from bedroom, and throw soggy pill away.

4) Take new pill from foil wrap, cradle cat in left arm holding rear paws tightly with left hand. Force jaws open and push pill to back of mouth with right forefinger. Hold mouth shut for a count of ten.

5) Retrieve pill from goldfish bowl and cat from top of wardrobe. Call spouse from garden.

6) Kneel on floor with cat wedged firmly between knees, hold front and rear paws. Ignore low growls emitted by cat. Get spouse to hold head firmly with one hand while forcing wooden ruler into mouth. Drop pill down the ruler and vigorously rub cat's throat.

7) Retrieve cat from curtain rail, get another pill from foil wrap. Make a note to buy new ruler and repair curtains. Carefully sweep shattered figurines and vases from hearth and set to one side for gluing later.

8) Wrap cat in large towel and get spouse to lie on cat with head just visible from below armpit. Put pill in end of drink-

ing straw, force mouth open with pencil and blow down drinking straw.

9) Check label to make sure pill is not harmful to humans, drink 1 beer to take taste away. Apply Band-Aid to spouse's forearm and remove blood from carpet with cold water and soap.

10) Retrieve cat from neighbor's shed. Get another pill. Open another beer. Place cat in cupboard and close door onto neck to leave head showing. Force mouth open with dessert spoon. Flick pill down throat with elastic band.

11) Fetch screwdriver from garage and put cupboard door back on hinges. Drink beer. Fetch bottle of Scotch. Pour shot, drink. Apply cold compress to cheek and check records for date of your last tetanus jab. Apply whiskey compress to cheek to disinfect. Toss back another shot. Throw tee-shirt away and fetch new one from bedroom.

12) Ring fire brigade to retrieve the friggin' cat from tree across the road. Apologize to neighbor who crashed into fence while swerving to avoid cat. Take last pill from foil wrap.

13) Tie the little b****'s front paws to rear paws with garden twine and bind tightly to leg of dining room table; find heavy duty pruning gloves from shed. Push pill into mouth followed by large piece of fillet steak. Be rough about it. Hold head vertically and pour 2 liters of water down throat to wash pill down.

14) Consume remainder of Scotch. Get spouse to drive you to the emergency room, sit quietly while doctor stitches fingers and forearm and removes pill remnants from right eye. Call furniture shop on way home to order new table.

15) Arrange for RSPCA to collect mutant cat from hell and ring local pet shop to see if they have any hamsters !

****

Dog:

Wrap pill in bacon, cheese or peanut butter. Make him beg!

I Want to Be a Bear ! ! !

- If you're a bear, you get to hibernate. You do nothing but sleep for Six Months.   I could deal with that.

- Before you hibernate, you're supposed to eat yourself stupid. I Could deal with that, too.

- If you're a bear, you birth your children (who are the size of walnuts) while you're sleeping and wake to partially grown, cute, cuddly cubs.
  I could definitely deal with that.

- If you're a Mama Bear, everyone knows you mean business. You swat anyone who bothers your cubs. If your cubs get out of line, you swat them too,
  I could deal with that.

- If you're a bear, your mate EXPECTS you to wake up growling. He EXPECTS that you will have hairy legs and excess body fat.

- **Yup** .... I wanna be a bear ! ! !

Chapter VII

POLITICIANS, POLITICS
And
THOUGHTS OF 9 / 11

Remember & Pray ....

"Please remember every one of the 300,000 (American) young men and women who are out here. I have never seen such a group of first class people....really, the best we have to offer.
Please pray for their safe return to their families and please pray that they do not harm the innocent. That is really high on everyone's minds here ... especially the military.

And pray for our country's future, that we may continue to be a beacon of hope and symbol of freedom throughout world. I am not so sure about it any more – that is why I ask you to pray ... HARD ... for it.

Regardless of one's stance toward this impending war ... I believe that we must keep in mind the American who, either by desire or direction, are in the Gulf and need our support ...

I know that our nation did not treat our returning Viet Nam veterans well, and we cannot allow ourselves to make the same errors with any of our military folks.

And those in the media – may we keep them in mind and pray for their safety."

There are obviously others – civilians and more – who will be in harms way, may we be able to pray for safety, and may we see soon the end of violence."

"Failure is the condiment that gives success its flavor."
Truman Capote, Author

The Soldier at Valley Forge in the Winter of 1777-1778

The Marquis de Lafayette wrote:

"The unfortunate soldiers were in want of everything; they had neither coats nor hats, nor shirts, nor shoes. Their feet and their legs froze until they were black, and it was often necessary to amputate them.

Over three months of shortage and extreme hardship were what over 11,000 soldiers endured.

The first priority of the soldiers was keeping warm and dry. The troops faced a typical Delaware Valley winter with temperatures mostly in the 20s and 30s. there were 13 days of rain or snow during the first six weeks. Illness, not musket balls, was the great killer.

Dysentery and typhus were rampant. Many makeshift hospitals were set up in the region. The Army's medical department used at least 50 barns, dwellings, churches, or meetinghouses throughout a wide area of Eastern Pennsylvania as temporary hospitals. These places were mostly understaffed, fetid breeding grounds of disease. All were chronically short of medical supplies.

It is estimated that over 3,000 soldiers died at Valley Forge and over 1,000 were far to ill to fight and had to be moved to medical facilities. The suffering and sacrifices of the American soldiers at Valley Forge are familiar, iconic images, but there is another side of the picture. Valley Forge was where a new, confident, professional American Army was born.

I want now you to close your eyes and picture in your mind this soldier at Valley Forge as he holds his musket in his bloody hands. He stands barefoot, feet bloody in the snow, starved from lack of food, wounded from months of battle and emotionally scarred from the eternity away from his family surrounded by nothing but death and carnage of war. He stands tough, with fire in his eyes and victory on his breath. He looks at us now in anger and disgust and tells us this:

>'I gave you a birthright of freedom, born in the constitution and now your children graduate too illiterate to read it.
>
>I fought barefoot and left bloody footprints in the snow to give you the freedom to vote and you stay at home because it rains.
>
>I left my family destitute to give you the freedom of speech and you remain silent on critical issues, because it might be bad for business, unpopular, or "politically incorrect.
>
>I orphaned my children to give you a government to serve you and it has stolen democracy from the people.
>
>It's the soldier, not the reporter, who gives you the freedom of the press.
>It's the soldier, not the poet, who gives you the freedom of speech.
>It's the soldier, not the campus organizer, who allows you to demonstrate.
>It's the soldier who salutes the flag, serves the flag, and whose coffin is draped with the flag that allows the protester to burn the flag ! ! !'

Gifts for our Troops

"Lord hold our troops in your loving hands. Protect them as they protect us. Bless them and their families for the selfless acts they perform for us in our time of need."

*Of all the gifts you could
give a member of the
United States Armed Forces,
Prayer is the very best one!*

FRENCH JOKES

"France has neither winter nor summer nor morals. Apart from these drawbacks, it is a fine country. France has usually been governed by prostitutes."

—Mark Twain

****

"I just love the French. They taste like chicken!"

—Hannibal Lecter

****

While speaking to the Hoover Institution today, Secretary Donald Rumsfeld was asked this question: "Could you tell us why to date at least the Administration doesn't favor direct talks with the North Korean government? After all, we're talking with the French."

The Secretary smiled and replied: "I'm not going there!"

****

"I would rather have a German division in front of me than a French one behind me."

— General George S. Patton

****

"Going to war without France is like going deer hunting without your accordion."

— Norman Schwartzkopf

****

What if Back in 1944?......"I dunno, let's send in some inspectors first, given 'em time to find out if the Germans are really as bad as they say."

****

"We can stand here like the French, or we can do something about it."

— Marge Simpson

****

"As far as I'm concerned, war always means failure"

—Jacques Chirac, President of France

****

"As far as France is concerned, you're right."

—Rush Limbaugh

****

"The only time France wants us to go to war is when the German Army is sitting in Paris sipping coffee."

—Regis Philbin

****

"There was a Frenchman, an Englishman and Claudia Schiffer sitting together in a carriage in a train going through Provence. Suddenly the train went through a tunnel and as it was an old style train, there were no lights in the carriages and it went completely dark. Then there was a kissing noise and the sound of a really loud slap.

When the train came out of the tunnel, Claudia Schiffer and the Englishman were sitting as if nothing had happened and the French-man had his hand against his face as if he had been slapped there.

The Frenchman was thinking 'The English fella must have kissed Claudia Schiffer and she missed him and slapped me instead.'

Claudia Schiffer was thinking 'The French fella must have tried to kiss me and actually kissed the Englishman and got slapped for it.'

And the Englishman was thinking 'This is great. The next time the train goes through a tunnel, I'll make another kissing noise and slap that French bastard again.'"

****

"The French are a smallish, monkey-looking bunch and not dressed any better, on average, than the citizens of Baltimore. True, you can sit outside in Paris and drink little cups of coffee, but why this is more stylish than sitting inside and drinking large glasses of whiskey I don't know"

— P. J. O'Rourke (1989)

****

" Next time there's a war in Europe, the loser has to keep France!"

****

An old saying: Raise your right hand if you like the French ; Raise both hands if you are French.

"You know, the French remind me a little bit of an aging actress of the 1940s who was still trying to dine out on her looks but doesn't have the face for it."

—John McCain, U.S. Senator from Arizona

****

"You know why the French don't want to bomb Saddam Hussein? Because he hates America, he loves mistresses and wears a beret. He *is* French, people."

—Conan O'Brien

****

"I don't know why people are surprised that France won't help us get Saddam out of Iraq. After all, France wouldn't help us get the Germans out of *France!*"

—Jay Leno

****

"The last time the French asked for 'more proof', it came marching into Paris under a German flag."

—David Letterman

REPLACEMENTS FOR THE
FRENCH NATIONAL ANTHEM:

"Runaway" by Del Shannon,
"Walk Right In" by the Rooftop singers,
"Everybody's Somebody's Fool" by Connie Francis,
"Running Scared" by Roy Orbison
"I Really Don't Want to Know" by Tommy Edwards,
"Surrender" by Elvis Presley,

"Save It For Me" by The Four Seasons,

"Live and Let Die" by the Wings,

"I'm Leaving it All Up to You" by Donny and Marie Osmond,

"What a Fool Believes" by the Doobie Brothers,

"Don't Worry, Be Happy" by Bobby McFerrin,

"Raise Your Hands" by Jon Bon Jovi.

# # # # # #

How many Frenchmen does it take to change a light bulb? One. He holds the bulb and all of Europe revolves around him!

# # # # # #

PROMISES! PROMISES!

After the 1993 World Trade Center bombing, which killed six and injured 1,000;
President Clinton promised that those responsible would be hunted down and punished.

After the 1995 bombing in Saudi Arabia, which killed five U.S. military personnel;
Clinton promised that those responsible would be hunted down and punished.

After the 1996 Khobar Towers bombing in Saudi Arabia, which killed nineteen and injured 200 U. S. military personnel;
Clinton promised that those responsible would be hunted down and punished.

After the 2000 bombing of the USS Cole, which killed seventeen and injured 39 U.S. sailors;
Clinton promised those responsible would be hunted down and punished.

Maybe if Clinton had kept his promises, an estimated 3,000 people in New York and Washington, D.C. that are now dead would be alive today.

And now that President Bush is taking action to bring these people to justice,
We have opponents charging him with being a war monger . . . .

An Interesting Question:

This question was raised on a Philly radio call-in show. Without casting stones, it is a legitimate question.

> There are two men, both extremely wealthy. One develops relatively cheap software and gives billions of dollars to charity. The other sponsors terrorism. That being the case, why was it that the Clinton Administration spent more money chasing down Bill Gates over the past eight years than Osama bin Laden ? ? ? ? ?

Think About It!

"It is a strange turn of events.
Hillary gets $8 Million for her forthcoming memoir.
Bill gets about $12 Million for his memoir yet to be written.
This from two people who have spent the past 8 years being unable to recall anything about past events while under oath!"

Cmdr Hamilton McWhorter
USN (ret)

"P.S. Please share this with as many people as you can! We don't want this woman to even THINK of running for President."

Remember: ☒ The Alamo   ☒ Pearl Harbor

☒ 9-11-01   ☒ The Clinton Years

All Truly American Disasters ! ! !

Truly an "All-Time Best Quote"

In a recent interview, General Norman Schwartzkopf was asked if he didn't think there was room for forgiveness toward the people who have harbored and abetted the terrorists who perpetrated the 9/11 attack on America.

His answer was classic. He said, *"I believe that forgiving them is God's function. Our job is simply to arrange that meeting as soon as possible."*

👍 👍 👍 👍 👍 👍 👍

Can you guess which politician that might be?

You really should be sitting down when you read this one. Gold Star Mothers is an organization made up of women whose sons were killed in military combat during service in the United States Armed Forces.

Recently a delegation of New York State Gold Star Mothers made a trip to Washington, DC to discuss various concerns with their elected representatives. According to published reports, there was only one politician who refused to meet with these ladies.

Can you guess which politician that might be? Was it New York Senator Charles Schumer? Nope, he met with them.

Try again, Do you know anyone serving in the Senate who has never showed anything but contempt for our military? Do you happen to know the name of any politician in Washington who's husband once wrote of his loathing for the military?

Now you're getting warm! You got it! None other than the queen herself, Hillary Clinton.
She refused repeated requests to meet with the Gold Star Mothers. Now, please don't tell me you're surprised.

This woman wants to be president of the United States – and there is a huge percentage of voters who are eager to help her achieve that goal.

> Sincerely,
> Cdr. Hamilton McWhorter
> USN (ret)

PS: Please share with as many people as you can. We don't want this woman to even think of running for President. May you sleep in peace always ... and please ... hug or thank a Veteran for that privilege.

Think About This One ! ! ! !

Don't forget, our girl, Hillary Rodham Clinton, as a New York Senator, now comes under this fancy Congressional Retirement and Staffing Plan. It's common knowledge that, in order for her to establish NYS residency, they purchased a million-plus dollar house in upscale Chappaqua, NY. Makes sense.

Now, they are entitled to Secret Service protection for life. Still makes sense. Here is where it becomes interesting. The mortgage payments are somewhere about $10,000 per month. BUT, an extra residence had to be built within the acreage in order to house the Secret Service agents. The Clinton's now charge the Secret Service $10,000 monthly rent for the use of said Secret Service residence and that amount is just about equal to their mortgage payment, meaning that **we, the tax payers, are paying the Clinton's mortgage, their transportation, their safety and security, their 12-man staff, and it's all perfectly legal!**

Osama Poem

Osama Bin Laden, your time is short;
We'd rather you die, than come to court.
Why are you hiding if it was in God's name?
You're just a punk with a turban; a pathetic shame.

I have a question, about your theory and laws;
"How com YOU never die for the cause?'
Is it because you're a coward who counts on others?
Well here in America, we stand by our brothers.

As is usual, you failed in your mission;
If you expected pure chaos, you can keep on wishin'.
Americans are now focused and stronger than ever;
Your death has become our next endeavor.

What you tried to kill, doesn't live in our walls;
It's not in buildings or shopping malls.
If all of our structures came crashing down;
It would still be there, safe and sound.

Because pride and courage can't be destroyed;
Even if the towers leave a deep void.
We'll band together and fill the holes
We'll bury our dead and bless their souls.

But then our energy will focus on you;
And you'll feel the wrath of the Red, White and the Blue.
So slither and hide like a snake in the grass;
Because America's coming to kick your ass ! ! ! !

David C. Powell, M.D.

An Article by Paul Harvey: *"Conveniently Forgotten Facts"*

Back in 1969 a group of Black Panthers decided that a fellow Black Panther named . . . Alex Rackley . . . needed to die. Rackley was suspected of disloyalty. Rackley was first tied to a chair. Once safely immobilized, his friends tortured him for hours by, among other things, pouring boiling water on him. When they got tired of torturing Rackley, Black Panther member, Warren Kimbo, took Rackley outside and put a bullet in his head. Rackley's body was later found floating in a river about 25 miles north of New Haven, Connecticut

Perhaps at this point, you're curious as to what happened to these Black Panthers. In 1977, that's only eight years later, only one of the killers was still in jail. The shooter, Warren Kimbro, managed to get a scholarship to Harvard, and became good friends with none other than Al Gore. He later became an assistant dean at an Eastern Connecticut State college. Isn't that something? As a '60s radical you can pump a bullet into someone's head, and a few years later, in the same state, you can become an assistant college dean!   *Only in America !*

Erica Huggins was the lady who served the Panthers by boiling the water for Mr. Rackley's torture. Some years later Ms. Huggins was elected to a California School Board.

How in the world do you think the killers got off so easy? Maybe it was in some part due to the efforts of two people who came to the defense of the Panthers. These two people actually went so far as to shut down Yale University with demonstrations in defense of the accused Black Panthers during their trial.

One of these people was none other than Bill Lan Lee. Mr. Lee, or Mr. Lan Lee, as the case may be, isn't a college dean. He isn't a member of a California School Board, He is now head of the U.S. Justice Department's Civil Rights Division, appointed by none other than Bill Clinton.

O.K., so who was the other Panther defender? Is this other notable Panther defender now a school board member? Is this other Panther apologist now an assistant college dean? No, neither!

The other Panther defender was, like Lee, a radical law student at Yale University at the time. She is now known as the "smartest woman in the world." She is none other than the Democratic Senator from the State of New York ———our former First Lady, the incredible Hillary Rodham Clinton.

And now, as Paul Harvey said;

You know *"the rest of the story"*.

Airline Humor

There are some conversations that passengers normally don't hear. The following are accounts of actual exchanges between airline pilots and control towers from around the world:

While taxiing, the crew of a US Air flight departing for Ft. Lauderdale made a wrong turn and came nose to nose with a United 727. The irate female ground controller lashed out at the US Air crew screaming "US Air 2771, where are you going? I told you to turn right onto Charlie taxiway! You turned right on Delta! Stop right there. I know it's difficult for you to tell the difference between C's and D's, but get it right!"

Continuing her tirade to the embarrassed crew, she was now shouting hysterically "God, you've screwed everything up! It'll take forever to sort this out! You stay right there and don't move 'til I tell you to! You can expect progressive taxi instructions in about half an hour and I want you to go exactly where I tell you, when I tell you, and how I tell you! You got that US Air 2771?"

"Yes ma'am," the humbled crew responded.

Naturally the ground control frequency went terribly silent after the verbal bashing of the US Air 2771. Nobody wanted to engage the irate ground controller in her current state. Tension in every cockpit at LGA was running high. Then an unknown pilot broke the silence and asked, "Wasn't I married to you once?"

The controller working a busy pattern told the 727 on downwind to make a three-sixty – do a complete circle, a move normally used to provide pacing between aircraft.

The pilot of the 727 complained "Don't you know it costs us two thousand dollars to make even a one-eighty in this airplane?"

Without missing a beat, the controller replied, "Roger, give me our thousand dollars worth."

A DC-10 had an exceedingly long rollout after landing with his approach speed a little high.

San Jose Tower: "American 751 heavy, turn right at the end of the runway, if able. If not able, take the Guadalupe exit off Highway 101 and make a right at the light to return to the airport."

Unknown Aircraft: "I'm f...ing bored!"
Air Traffic Control: "Last aircraft transmitting, identify yourself immediately!"
Unknown aircraft: "I said I was f...ing bored, not f...ing stupid!"

It was a really nice day, right about dusk, and a Piper Malibu was being vectored into a long line of airliners in order to land at Kansas city.

KC Approach: "Malibu three-two Charlie, you're following a 727, one o'clock and three miles."

Three-two Charlie: "We've got him. We'll follow him."

KC Approach: "Delta 105, your traffic to follow is a Malibu, eleven o'clock and three miles. Do you have that traffic?"

Delta 105 (in a thick southern drawl, after a long pause): "Well ... I've got something down there. Can't quite tell if it's a Malibu or a Chevelle."

Tower: "Eastern 702, cleared for takeoff, contact Departure on _____24.7."

Eastern 702: "Tower, Eastern 702 switching to Departure. By the way, after we lifted off, we saw some kind of dead animal on the far end of the runway."

Tower: "Continental 635, cleared for takeoff, contact Departure ____24.7. Did you copy that report from Eastern?"

Continental 635: Continental 635, cleared for takeoff, roger; and yes, we copied Eastern and we've already notified our caterers.

The German air controllers at Frankfurt Airport are a short-tempered lot. They not only expect one to know one's gate parking location, but how to get there without any assistance from them. So it was with some amusement that we (a Pan Am 747) listened to the following exchange between Frankfurt ground control and a British Airways 747, call sign "Speedbird 206":

Speedbird 206: "Top of the morning, Frankfurt, Speedbird 206 clear of the active runway."

Ground: "Guten Morgen. You vill taxi to your gate."

The big British Airways 747 pulled onto the main taxiway and slowed to a stop.

Ground: "Speedbird, do you not know where you are going?"

Speedbird 206: "Stand by a moment, Ground, I'm looking up our gate location now."
Ground (with arrogant impatience): "Speed bird 206, haff you never flown to Frankfurt before?"

Speedbird 206 (coolly): "Yes, I have, actually, in 1944. In another type of Boeing, but just to drop something off. I didn't land."

O'Hare Approach Control: "United 329 heavy, your traffic is a Fokker, one o'clock,
three miles eastbound."
United 239: "Approach, I've always wanted to say this … I've got that Fokker in sight."

A Pan AM 727 flight engineer waiting for start clearance in Munich overheard the following:
    Lufthansa (in German): Ground, what is our start clearance time?"

Ground (in English): "If you want an answer you must speak English."

Lufthansa (in English): "I am a German, flying a German airplane, in Germany. Why must I speak English?"

Unknown voice (in a beautiful British accent): "Because you lost the bloody war!"

"Lincoln's Cannots"

You cannot bring about prosperity by discouraging thrift.

You cannot strengthen the weak by weakening the strong.

You cannot help small men by tearing down big men.

You cannot help the poor by destroying the rich.

You cannot lift the wage earner by pulling down the wage payer.

You cannot keep out of trouble by spending more than your income.

You cannot further brotherhood of men by inciting class hatred.

You cannot build character and courage by taking away a man's initiative.
You cannot really help men by having the government tax them to do what they can and should do for themselves.

Similarities between Nixon and Clinton

Nixon: Watergate
Clinton: Waterbed

Nixon: His biggest fear – the Cold War
Clinton: His biggest fear – a Cold sore

Nixon: Worried about carpet bombs
Clinton: Worried about carpet burns

Nixon: His Vice President was a Greek
Clinton: His Vice President was a geek

Nixon: Couldn't stop Kissinger
Clinton: Couldn't stop kissing her

Nixon: Couldn't explain the 18 minute gap in the Watergate
          tape
Clinton: Couldn't explain the 36DD braw in his brief case

Nixon: His nickname was Tricky Dick
Clinton: Same

Nixon: Ex-President
Clinton: Sex-President

Nixon: Known for campaign slogan "Nixon's The One"
Clinton: Known for women pointing at him saying, "He's the
          one!"

Nixon: Famous for his widow's peak
Clinton: Famous for bringing widows to their peak
Nixon: Well acquainted with G. Gordon Liddy
Clinton: Well acquainted with the G Spot

Nixon:	Took on Ho Chi Minh
Clinton:	Took on Ho

Nixon:	Talked about achieving peace with honor
Clinton:	Talked about getting a piece while on her

Two Thousand One, Nine Eleven

Two thousand one, nine eleven
Five thousand plus arrive in heaven
As they pass through the gate,   .
Thousands more appear in wait
A bearded man with stovepipe hat
Steps forward saying, "Let's sit, lets chat".

They settle down in seats of clouds
A man named Martin shouts out proud
"I have a dream!" and once he did
The Newcomer said, "Your dream still lives."

Groups of soldiers in blue and gray
Others in khaki, and green then say
"We're from Bull Run, Yorktown, the Maine"
The Newcomer said, "You died not in vain."

From a man on sticks one could hear
"The only thing we have to fear..."
The Newcomer said, "We know the rest,
Trust us sir, we've passed that test"

"Courage doesn't hide in caves
You can't bury freedom, in a grave."
The Newcomer had heard this voice before
A distinct Yankee's twang from Hyannis port shores.

A silence fell within the mist
Somehow the Newcomer knew that this
Meant time had come for her to say
What was in the hearts of the five thousand plus that day.

"Back on Earth, we wrote reports,
Watched our children play in sports
Worked our gardens, sang our songs
Went to church and clipped coupons
We smiled, we laughed, we cried, we fought
Unlike you, great we're not."

The tall man in the stovepipe hat
Stood and said, "Don't talk like that!
Look at your country, look and see
You died for freedom, just like me."

Then, before them all appeared a scene
Of rubbled streets and twisted beams
Death, destruction, smoke and dust
And people working just 'cause they must.

Hauling ash, lifting stones,
Knee deep in hell, but not alone
"Look! Black man, White man, Brown man, Yellow man
Side-by-side helping their fellow man!"

So said Martin, as he watched the scene
"Even from nightmares, can be born a dream."

Down below three firemen raised
The colors high into ashen haze
The soldiers above had seen it before
On Iwo Jima back in '44.
The man on sticks studied everything closely
Then shared his perceptions on what he saw mostly
"I see pain, I see tears,

I see sorrow – but I don't see fear."

"You left behind husbands and wives
Daughters and sons and so many lives
Are suffering now because of this wrong
But look very closely. You're not really gone.

All of those people, even those who've never met you
All of their lives, they'll never forget you
Don't you see what has happened?
Don't you see what you've done?
You've brought them together, together as one."

With that the man in the stovepipe hat said
"Take my hand," and from there he led
Five thousand plus heroes, Newcomers to heaven
On this day, two thousand one, nine eleven.

Iraqi Facts

What is the Iraqi air force motto?
I came, I saw, Iran.

Have you heard about the new Iraqi air force exercise program?
Each morning you raise your hands above your head and leave
them there.

What's the five-day forecast for Baghdad?
Two days.

What do Miss Muffet and Saddam Hussein have in common?
They both have Kurds in their way.

What is the best Iraqi job?
Foreign ambassador.

Did you hear that it is twice as easy to train Iraqi fighter pilots?

You only have to teach them to take off.
How do you play Iraqi bingo?   B-52 .... F-16 ......B-52 .....

What is Iraq's national bird?
Duck.

What do Saddam Hussein and General Custer have in common?
They both want to know where the hell those Tomahawks are coming from!

Why does the Iraqi navy have glass bottom boats?
So they can see their air force.

Chapter VIII

COMPUTERS . . . . . ENOUGH SAID!

David C. Powell, M.D.

Remember When . . . .

A computer was something on TV
From a science fiction show
A window was something you hated to clean....
And Ram was the cousin of a goat . . . .

Meg was the name of my girlfriend
And gig was your middle finger upright
Now they all mean different things
And that really mega bytes.

An application was for employment
A program was a TV show
A cursor used profanity
A keyboard was a piano.

Memory was something that you lost with age
A CD was a bank account
And if you had a 3" floppy
You hoped nobody found out.

Compress was something you did to the garbage
Not something you did to a file
And if you unzipped anything in public
You'd be in jail for a while.

Log on was adding wood to the fire
Hard drive was a long trip on the road
A mouse pad was where a mouse lived
And a backup happened to your commode.

Cut you did with a pocket knife
Paste you did with glue
A web was a spider's home
And a virus was the flu.

I guess I'll stick to my pad and paper
And the memory in my head
I hear nobody's been killed in a computer crash
But when it happens they wish they were dead.

We all know those cute little computer symbols called "emoticons, " where :) means a smile and :(is a frown. Sometimes these are represented by :-) and :- (respectively. Well, how about some "ass-cons"?

Here goes:

(_!_)	a regular ass	(_o_)	an ass that's been around
(__!__)	a fat ass	(_O_)	an ass that's been around even more
(!)	a tight ass	(_x_)	kiss my ass
(_._)	a flat ass	(_X_)	leave my ass alone
(_^_)	a bubble ass	(_zzz_)	a tired ass
(_*_)	a sore ass	(_o^o_)	a wise ass
(_!__)	a lop-sided ass	(_13_)	an unlucky ass
{_!_}	a swishy ass	(_$_)	money coming out of his ass
		(_?_)	dumb ass

What a Dilemma!

A retired sailor purchased a computer and began to learn all about computing. Being a sailor, he was used to addressing his ships as

"She" or "Her". But was unsure what was proper for computers. To solve his dilemma, he found two groups of computer experts: one group was male, and the other was female.

The group of women reported that computers should be referred to as "HE" because:

1) In order to get their attention you have to turn them on.
2) They have a lot of data but are still clueless.
3) They are supposed to help you solve problems but half the time they are the problem.
4) As soon as you commit to one, you realize that if you had waited a little longer, you could have had a newer and better model.

The group of men reported that computers should be referred to as "SHE" because:

1) No one but the creator understands their logic.
2) The native language they use to talk to other computers is incomprehensible to anyone else.
3) Even your smallest mistakes are stored in long term memory for later retrieval.
4) As soon as you make a commitment to one, you find yourself spending half your paycheck on accessories for it.

Why the Internet is Like a Penis.

❖ It can be up or down. It's more fun when it's up, but that makes it difficult to get any real work done.
❖ In the long-distant past, its only purpose was to transmit information considered vital to the survival of the species. Some people still think that's the only thing it should be used for, but most folks today use it for fun most of the time.

- ❖ It has no conscience and no memory. Left to its own devices, it will just do the same damn dumb things it did before.

- ❖ It provides a way to interact with other people. Some people take this interaction very seriously, others treat it as a lark. Sometimes it's hard to tell what kind of person you're dealing with until it's too late.

- ❖ If you don't apply the appropriate protective measures, it can spread viruses.

- ❖ It has no brain of its own. Instead, it uses yours. If you use it too much, you'll find it becomes more and more difficult to think coherently.

- ❖ We attached an importance to it that is far greater than its actual size and influence warrant.

- ❖ If you're not careful what you do with it, it can get you in big trouble.

- ❖ It has its own agenda. Somehow, no matter how good your intentions, it will warp your behavior. Later you may ask yourself "why on earth did I do that?"

- ❖ Some folks have it, some don't.

- ❖ Those who have it would be devastated if it were ever cut off. They think that those who don't have it are somehow inferior. They think it gives them power. They are wrong. Those who don't have it may agree that it's a nifty toy, but think it's not worth the fuss that those who do have it make about it. Still, many of those who don't have it would like to try it.

- ❖ Once you've started playing with it, it's hard to stop. Some people would just play with it all day if they didn't have work to do.

Dear Dell Tech Support:

Last year I upgraded from Boyfriend 5.0 to Husband 1.0 and noticed a slow-down in the performance of the flower and jewelry applications that had operated flawlessly under the boyfriend 5.0 system.

In addition, Husband 1.0 uninstalled many other valuable programs, such as romance 9.9, but installed undesirable programs such as NFL 7.4, NBA d.2 and NHL 4.1. conversation 8.0 also no longer runs and Housecleaning 2.6 simply crashes the system. I've tried running Nagging 5.3 to fix these problems, but to no avail.

What can I do?

"Desperately Seeking Solution"

Dear Desperately Seeking Solution,

First, keep in mind that Boyfriend 5.0 was an entertainment package, while Husband 1.0 is an operating system.

Try to enter the command C:/I THOUGHT YOU LOVE ME AND INSTALL tears 6.2. Husband 1.0 should then automatically run the applications: guilt 3.3 and Flowers 7.5. but remember overuse can cause Husband 1.0 to default to such background applications as Grumpy Silence 2.5, Happy Hour 7.0, or Beer 6.1.

Please remember that Beer 6.1 is a very bad program that will create Snoring Loudly.WAV files. DO NOT install Mother-In-Law 1.0 or reinstall another Boyfriend program. These are not supported applications and will crash Husband 1.0. it could also potentially cause Husband 1.0 to default to the program: Girlfriend 9.2, which runs in the background and has been known to introduce potentially serious viruses into the Operating system.

In summary, Husband 1.0 is a great program, but it does have limited memory and can't learn new applications quickly. You might consider buying additional software to enhance his system performance. I personally recommend Hot Food 3.0 and single Malt Scotch 4.5 combined with such applications as Boob Job 3.6D and that old

standby . . . Lingerie 6.9 (which have both been credited with improved performance of his hardware).

Good Luck,
Dell Tech Support

****

THE COMPUTER MESSAGE "Bad command or File Name" is about
as informative as "If you don't know why I'm mad at you, then I'm
certainly not going to tell you."

****

Technology for Country Folk . . . .

1)	LOG ON:	Making a wood stove hotter
2)	LOG OFF:	Don't add no more wood.
3)	MONITOR:	Keep'n an eye on the wood stove.
4)	DOWNLOAD:	Getting the farwood off the truk.
5)	MEGA HERTZ:	When yer not kerful getting the farwood.
6)	FLOPPY DISC:	Whatcha git from tryin to carry too much farwood.
7)	RAM:	That thar thing whut splits the farwood.
8)	HARD DRIVE:	Getting home in the winter time.
9)	PROMPT:	What the mail ain't in the winter time.
10)	WINDOWS:	Whut to shut wen it's cold outside.
11)	SCREEN:	Whut to shut wen it's blak fly season.
12)	BYTE:	Whut them dang flys do.
13)	CHIP:	Munchies fer the TV.
14)	MICRO CHIP:	Whut's in the bottom of the munchie bag.
15)	MODEM:	What cha did to the hay fields.

16) DOT MATRIX: Old Dan Matrix's wife.
17) LAP TOP: Whar the kitty sleeps.
18) KEYBOARD: Whar ya hang the dang keys.
19) SOFTWARE: Them dang plastic forks and knifes.
20) MOUSE: Whut eats the grain in the barn.
21) MAINFRAME: Holds up the barn roof.
22) PORT: Fancy Flatlander wine.
23) ENTER: Northerner talk fer "C'mon in y'all"
24) MOUSE PAD: Where Mickey and Minnie live
25) RANDOM ACCESS
    MEMORY: Wen ya cain't 'member what ya paid
                    fer the rifle when yore wife asks.
26) BACKUP: What you do when you run across a
                    skunk in the woods.
27) BUG: The reason you give for calling in
                    sick
28) CACHE: Needed when you run out of food
                    stamps.
29) TERMINAL: Time to call the undertaker.
30) CRASH: When you go to Junior's party
                    uninvited.
31) DIGITAL: The art of counting on your fingers.
32) DISKETTE: Female Disco dancer.
33) FAX: What you lie about to the IRS.
34) HACKER: Uncle /Leroy after 32 years of
                    smoking.
35) HARDCOPY: Picture looked at when selecting
                    tattoos.
36) INTERNET: Where cafeteria workers put their
                    hair.
37) MAC: Big Bubba's favorite fast food.
38) ON LINE: Where to stay when taking the
                    sobriety test.
39) ASCII: What you call your week-old
                    underwear.

New Virus Warning:

This is deadly serious, so don't ignore it. Several new viruses have been discovered and are wreaking havoc throughout the national system. Beware of :

THE CLINTON virus .... Gives you a 6-inch hard Drive with No memory.

THE BOB DOLE (a.k.a. VIAGRA) virus .... Makes a new hard drive out of an old floppy.

THE LEWINSKY virus .... Sucks all the memory out of your computer, then e-mails everyone about what it did.

THE RONALD REAGAN virus .... Saves your data, but forgets where it is stored.

THE MIKE TYSON virus .... Quits after two bytes.

THE OPRAH WINFREY virus ....Your 300mg hard drive shrinks to 100mg, then slowly expands to stabilize around 200 mg.

THE JACK KAVORKIAN virus .... Deletes all old files.

THE ELLEN DEGENERES virus .... Disks can no longer be inserted.

THE PROZAC virus ....Totally screws up your RAM, but your processor doesn't care.

THE JOEY BUTTAFUOCO virus.... Only attacks minor files.

THE ARNOLD SCHWARZENEGGER virus...Terminates some files, leaves but will be back.

And last but not least ......

THE LINDA BOBBIT virus .... Reformats your hard drive into a 3.5 inch floppy, then discards it through Windows.

Dear Tech Support:

Last year I upgraded Girlfriend 1.0 to Wife 1.0 and noticed that the new program began unexpected child processing that took up a lot of space and valuable resources. No mention of this phenomenon was included in the product brochure.

In addition, Wife 1.0 installs itself into other programs and launches during system initialization where it monitors all other system activity. Applications such as Pokernight 10.3 and Beerbash2.5 no longer run, crashing the system whenever selected. I cannot seem to purge Wife 1.0 from my system.

I am thinking about going back to Girlfriend 1.0 but uninstall does not work on this program. Can you help?

Jonathan Powell

===

Dear Jon,

This is a very common problem men complain about but is mostly due to a primary misconception.

Many people upgrade from Girlfriend 1.0 to Wife 1.0 with the idea that Wife 1.0 is merely a "UTILITIES & ENTERTAINMENT" program. In fact, Wife 1.0 is an OPERATING SYSTEM and designed by it's creator to run everything. It is impossible to uninstall, delete or purge the program from the system once installed.

You can not go back to a Girlfriend 1.0 because Wife 1.0 is not designed to do this. Some have tried to install Girlfriend 2.0 or Wife 2.0 but end up with more problems than original system. Look in your manual under WARNINGS: Alimony/Child Support. I recommend you keep Wife 1.0 and just deal with the situation.

Having Wife 1.0 installed myself, I might also suggest you read the entire section regarding General Protection Faults (GPFs). You must assume all responsibility for faults and problems that might occur. The best course of action will be to push the apologize button then reset button as soon as lock-up occurs. System will run smooth as long as you take blame for all GPFs. Wife 1.0 is a great program but is very high maintenance.

Answer Man

Chapter IX

REDNECKS, SOUTHERNERS, et. al.

With all credit to Jeff Foxworthy for any of the "Rednecks" that he might have done; to Lewis Grizzard (rest in peace) for his Redneck soul; and to all the other Rednecks who came up with these and passed them on by word of mouth since most of us can't read anyway.....

Southern Charm

Issued by the Southern Tourism Bureau to ALL visiting Northerners and Northeastern Urbanites:

1) Don't order filet mignon or pasta primavera at Waffle House. It's just a diner. They serve breakfast 24 hours-a-day. Let them cook something they know. If you confuse them, they'll kick your ass.

2) Don't laugh at our southern names (Marleen, Bodie, Ovine, Luther Ray, Tammy Lynn, Darla Beth, Inez, Billy Joe, Sissy, Clovis, etc.) or we will just HAVE to kick your ass.

3) Don't order a bottle of pop or a can of soda down here. Down here it's called Coke. Nobody gives a flying damn whether it's Pepsi, RC, Dr. Pepper, 7-Up or whatever – it's still a coke. Accept it. Doing otherwise can lead to an ass kicking.

4) We know our heritage. Most of us are more literate than you (e.g., Welty, Williams, Faulkner). We are also better educated and generally a lot nicer. Don't refer to us as a bunch of hillbillies, or we'll kick your ass.

5) We have plenty of business sense (e.g., Fred Smith of Fed Ex, Turner Broadcasting, MCI WorldCom, MTV Netscape). Naturally, we do, sometimes have small lapses in judgment (e.g., Carter, Edwards, Duke Barnes, Clinton). We don't care if you think we are dumb. We are not dumb enough to let someone move to our state in order to run for the Senate. If someone tried to do that, we would kick their ass.

6) Don't laugh at our Civil War monuments. If Lee had listened to Longstreet and flanked Meade at Gettysburg instead of sending Pickett up the middle, you'd be paying taxes to Rich-

mond instead of Washington. If you visit Stone Mountain and complain about the carving, we'll kick your ass.

7) We are fully aware of how high the humidity is, so shut the hell up. Just spend your money and get the hell out of here, or we'll kick your ass.

8) Don't order wheat toast at Cracker Barrel. Everyone will instantly know that you're a Yankee. Eat your biscuits like God intended – with gravy. And don't put sugar on your grits, or we'll kick your ass.

9) You try to take a southern accent, this will incite a riot, and you will get your ask kicked.

10) Don't talk about how much better things are at home because we know better. Many of us have visited Northern shitholes like Detroit, Chicago, and DC, and we have the scars to prove it. If you don't like it here, Delta is ready when you are. Move your ass on home before it gets kicked.

11) Yes, we know how to speak proper English. We talk this way because we don't want to sound like you. We don't care if you don't understand what we are saying. All other southerners understand what we are saying, and that's all that matters. Now, go away and leave us alone, or we'll kick your ass.

12) Don't complain that the South is dirty and polluted. None of our lakes or rivers have caught fire recently. If you whine about our scenic beauty, we'll kick your ass all the way back to Boston Harbor.

13) Don't ridicule our southern manners. We say "sir" and "ma'am". We hold doors open for others. We offer our seats to old folks because such things are expected of civilized people. Behave yourselves around our sweet little gray-

haired grandmothers or they'll kick some manners into your ass just like they did ours.

14) So you think we're quaint or losers because most of us live in the countryside? That's because we have enough sense to not live in filthy, smelly, crime-infested cesspools like New York or Baltimore. Make fun of our fresh air, and we'll kick your ass.

15) Last, but not least, DO NOT DARE TO COME DOWN HERE AND TELL US HOW TO COOK BARBECUE. This will get your ass shot (right after it is kicked). You're lucky we let you come down here at all. Criticize our barbeque, and you will go home in a pine box, minus your ass!.

You Know You're from North Carolina if:

➤ You measure distance in minutes.

➤ Down East to you means east of Raleigh.

➤ Down South means South Carolina.

➤ You know a bunch of people who have hit a deer.

➤ If you know a few that have also hit a bear.

➤ You have no problem spelling or pronouncin' "Conetoe" or "Topsail:".

➤ Your school classes were canceled because of cold.

➤ Your school classes were canceled because of heat.

➤ Your school classes were canceled because of a hurricane.

➤ Your school classes were canceled because of hunting.

➤ Your school classes were canceled because of a livestock show.

➤ You've ridden the school bus for an hour... each way.

➤ You know "the word" and "the price".

➤ You've ever had to switch from "Heat" to "A/C" in the same day.

➤ You think ethanol makes your truck run a lot better.

➤ Stores don't have bags . . . they have sacks and are called Piggly Wigglys.

➤ You see people wearing bib overalls at funerals.

➤ You see a car running in the parking lot at the store with no one in it no matter what time of the year.

➤ You end your sentences with a preposition, for example, "Where's my coat at?" "What's that made out of?"

➤ All the festivals around the state are named after a fruit, vegetable, or politician.

➤ Priming was your first job . . . and you know what it means.

➤ Your idea of a really great tenderloin is when the meat is twice as big as the bun and comes with cole slow on top.

➤ You put security lights on your house and your garage and leave both of them unlocked.

➤ You think the four major food groups are beef, pork, beer, and Jello salad with marshmallows.

➤ When asked how your trip to any foreign, exotic place was, you say "It was different"

➤ Hyde county is considered a foreign or exotic place.

➤ You carry jumper cables in your car.

➤ You know the following: Duke - Smart A—, State – Farmer's Kids, Carolina – Preps, ECU-Drunks.

➤ You faithfully drink Pepsi or Mt. Dew everyday of your life.

➤ You know what "cow tipping" is.

➤ You have your own secret barbecue sauce.

➤ You or your neighbors have more hunting dogs than you have family members.

➤ You visit the NC State Fair mainly to see your neighbor's prize.

Redneck Song Titles:

❖ Get Your Tongue Out'ta My mouth 'Cause I'm Kissing you Goodbye

❖ (Pardon Me) I've got someone to Kill

❖ I Got In At Two, With a Ten and Woke Up at Ten with a Two

❖ If the Jukebox took Teardrops, I'd Cry All Night Long

❖ I don't Know Whether to come Home or Go Crazy

❖ Her Body couldn't Keep You off my Mind

❖ Her Cheatin' Heart Made a Drunken Fool Out of Me

❖ Out of My Head and Back in My Bed

❖ You're a Cross I Can't Bear

❖ It don't Feel Like Sinnin' To Me

❖ I'm Getting' Gray From Being Blue

❖ I Keep Forgettin' I Forgot About You

❖ You Hurt the Love Right Out of Me

❖ Mama Get the Hammer (There's A Fly on Papa's Head)

❖ Heaven's Just a sin Away

❖ She Made Toothpicks Out of the Timber of My Heart

❖ Get Your Biscuits in the Oven and Your Buns in the Bed

❖ You're the Reason Our Kids Are So Ugly

❖ Guess My Eyes were Bigger Than my Heart

❖ If Fingerprints Shows Up on Skin, wonder Whose I'd Find on You

❖ I Don't Know Whether to Kill Myself or go Bowling

❖ If Whiskey Were a Woman, I'd be Married for Sure

❖ It Ain't Love but It ain't Bad

❖ I've Been Flushed From the Bathroom of Your Heart

❖ She Feels Like a New Man Tonight

❖ I May be Used (But Baby I Ain't Used Up)

❖ I'm the Only Hell Mama Ever Raised

❖ If Drinkin' don't Kill Me, Her Memory Will

❖ Velcro Arms, Teflon Heart

❖ If you Can't Feel it (It Ain't There)

❖ Touch Me with More Than Your Hands

❖ I've Got the Hungries for your Love and I'm Waiting In Your Welfare Line

❖ The Last Word In Lonesome Is "ME"

❖ Do you Love as Good as You Look

❖ I'll Marry You tomorrow, but Let's Honeymoon Tonight

❖ When we Get Back to the Farm (That's When We Really Go to Town)

❖ My Shoes Keep Walkin' Back to You

❖ You Stuck My Heart in a Old Tin Can and Shot It Off a Log

❖ And there was Grandma, Swingin' on the Outhouse Door, without a Shirt On

❖ How Can I Miss You When You won't Go Away? (I keep on seeing you, day after day; You never leave here, you always stay and stay. How can I Miss You When You won't Go Away?)

❖ Why do you Believe me when I Tell You That I Love You When You Know I've Been a Liar all my Life?

❖ He's Been Drunk Since His Wife's Gone Punk

Southern Signs

What's Your "Southern" Sign? Some of us (especially Southerners) are pretty skeptical of horoscopes, and it has become obvious that what we need are "Southern" symbols:

OKRA (Dec 22 – Jan. 20) – Although you appear crude, you are actually very slick on the inside. Okras have tremendous influence. An older Okra can look back over his life and see the seeds of his influence everywhere. Stay away from Moon Pies.

CHITLIN' (Jan. 21 – Feb. 19) – Chitlin's come from humble backgrounds. A chitlin', however, can make something of himself if he's motivated and has lots of seasoning. In dealing with Chitlin's, be careful. They can erupt like Vesuvius. Chitlin's are best with Catfish and Okra.

BOLL WEEVIL (Feb. 20 – Mar. 20) –You have an overwhelming curiosity. You're unsatisfied with the surface of things, and you feel the need to bore deep into the interior of everything. Needless to say, you are very intense and driven as if you had some inner hunger. Nobody in their right mind is going to marry you, so don't worry about it.

NOON PIE (Mar. 21 – Apr. 20) –You're the type that spends a lot of time on the front porch. It's a cinch to recognize the physical appearance of Moon Pies. Big and round are the key words here. You should marry anybody who you can get remotely interested in the idea. It's not going to be easy. This might be the year to think about aerobics. Or – maybe not.

POSSUM (Apr. 21 – May 21) –When confronted with life's difficulties, possums have a marked tendency to withdraw and develop a don't-bother-me-about-it attitude. Sometimes you become so withdrawn, people actually think you're dead. This strategy is probably not psychologically healthy, but seems to work for you. One day, however, it won't work and you may find your problems actually running you over.

CRAWFISH (May 22 – Jun, 21) – Crawfish is a water sign. If you work in an office, you're always hanging around the water cooler. Crawfish prefer the beach to the mountains, the pool to the golf course, the bathtub to the living room. You tend to be not particularly attractive physically, but you have very, very good heads.

COLLARDS (Jun. 22 – Jul. 23) – Collards have a genius for communication. They love to get in the "melting pot" of life and share their essence with the essence of those 'round them. Collards make good social workers, psychologists, and baseball managers. As far as your personal life goes, if you are Collards, stay away from Moon Pies. It just won't work. Save yourself a lot of heartache.

CATFISH (Jul. 24 – Aug. 23) – Catfish are traditionalists in matters of the heart, although one with whiskers may cause problems for loved ones. You catfish are never easy people to understand. You prefer the muddy bottoms to the clear surface of life. Above all else, Catfish should stay away from Moon Pies.

GRITS (Aug. 24 – Sept. 23) –Your highest aim is to be with others like yourself. You like to huddle together with a big crowd of other Grits. You love to travel though, so maybe you should think about joining a club. Where do you like to go? Anywhere they have cheese or gravy or bacon or butter or eggs. If you can go somewhere where they have all these things, that serves you well.

BOILED PEANUTS (Sep. 24 – Oct. 23) – You have passionate desire to help your fellow man. Unfortunately, those who know you best – your friends and loved ones – may find that your personality is much too salty, and their criticism will probably affect you deeply because you are really much softer that you appear. You should go right ahead and marry anybody you want to because in a certain way, yours is a charmed life. On the road of life, you can be sure that people will always pull over and stop for you.

BUTTER BEAN (Oct. 24 – Nov. 22) – Always invite a Butter Bean because Butter Beans get along well with everybody. You, as a Butter Bean, should be proud. You've grown on the vine of life and you feel at home no matter what the setting. You can sit next to anybody. However, you, too, shouldn't have anything to do with Moon Pies.

ARMADILLO (Nov. 23 – Dec. 21) – You have a tendency to develop a tough exterior, but you are actually quite gentle. A good evening for you? Old friends, a fire, some roots, fruit, worms and insects. You are a throwback. You're not concerned with today's fashions and trends. You're not concerned with anything about today. You're really almost prehistoric in your interests and behavior patterns. You probably want to marry another Armadillo, but Possum is another somewhat kinky, mating possibility.

You Know You're a Redneck if ....

< The Halloween pumpkin on your front porch has more teeth than your spouse.

< You let your twelve year old daughter smoke at the dinner table in front of her kids.

< Last year you hid Easter eggs under cow pies.

< You've been married three times and still have the same in-laws.

< You think a woman who is "out of your league" bowls on a different night.

< Jack Daniels makes your list of "Most Admired People."

< You think Genitalia is an Italian airline.

< You wonder how service stations keep their restrooms so clean.

< Anyone in your family ever died right after saying "Hey, yall, watch this!"

< You think that Dom Perignon is a Mafia leader.

< You go to your family reunion looking for a date.

< Your Junior / Senior Prom had a Daycare.

< You think the last words to The Star Spangled Banner are, "Gentlemen, start your engines."

< You lit a match in the bathroom and your house exploded right off it's wheels.

< The bluebook value of your truck goes up and down, depending on how much gas it has in it.

< You need one more hole punched in your card to get a freebie at the House of Tattoos.

Work is The Curse of the Drinking Classes...

While most companies refrain from allowing consumption of alcohol on the premises, there are some arguments for changing that policy.

Reasons for allowing drinking at work include:

} It's an incentive to show up.

} It reduces stress.

} It leads to more honest communications.

} It reduces complaints about low pay.

} It cuts down on time off because you can work with a hangover.

} Employees tell management what they think, not what they want to hear.

} It helps save on heating costs in the winter.

} It encourages carpooling.

} Increases job satisfaction because if you have a bad job, you don't care

} It eliminates vacations because people would rather come to work.

} It makes fellow employees look better.

} It makes the cafeteria food taste better.

} Bosses are more likely to hand out raises when they are wasted.

⟩ Salary negotiations are a lot more profitable.

⟩ Suddenly, farting during a meeting isn't so embarrassing.

How Southerners Really Feel About "Yankees" !

A Southerner is having his breakfast of coffee, grits, biscuits when a Northerner, chewing obnoxiously on gum, sits down next to the Southerner. The Southerner ignores the Northerner who, nevertheless, starts conversation:

Northerner: "When you Southern people eat bread, do you eat the crusts?"
Southerner: "Yep."
Northerner: (After blowing a huge bubble with that gum) "We don't, up North we eat what's inside. The crusts we collect in a container, recycle it, transform them into biscuits and send them to the South."
The Northerner has a smirk on his face.
The Southerner listens in silence.
The Northerner persists: "Do you eat jam with biscuits?"
Southerner: "Yep."
Northerner: (Cracking and smacking his gum between his teeth and lips) "We don't. Up North, after we eat fruit for breakfast, we put all the seeds and leftovers in containers, recycle them, transform them, then send it down South."
The Southerner asks, "Y'all have sex up North?"
Northerner: "Why, of course, we do." And he pops another big bubble.
Southerner: "And what do y'all do with the condoms once ya use them?"
Northerner: "We throw them away, of course."
Southerner: "We don't. Down South, we put 'em in a jar, melt 'em and make bubble gum, and sell it to Yankees."

Top Ten Signs You're at a Redneck Wedding:

10. Rehearsal dinner is held at Hooter's.

9. Instead of "Friends of the Bride or Friends of the Groom." The ushers asks, "Ford or Chevy"?

8. Bridesmaids pick tube tops; bridegrooms choose Travis Tritt T-shirts.

7. Phrase, "I Do" is replaced by "I heard That".

6. Tender rendition of the wedding song performed by Cledus T. Judd.

5. The minister asks, "Who giveth this woman to be married?", and some guy in the back of the church stands up and yells, "Earnhardt!".

4. Reception conversation includes, "So what'cha been doing since Hee Haw, Mr. Lindsay?"

3. Snack trays at the reception: Vienna sausages and nacho cheese Doritos.

2. Plans for the honeymoon evening include tickets to the Monster Truck Show.

And the number one sign that you're at a
Redneck Wedding .....

 # 1. Sign at the front of the church reads, "No shoes, No shirt, No PROBLEM!"

40 Things Never Said by Southerners

40. Oh I just couldn't. Hell, she's only sixteen.

39. I'll take Shakespeare for 1000, Alex.

38. Duct tape won't fix that.

37. Lisa Marie was lucky to catch Michael.

36. Come to think of it, I'll have a Heineken.

35. We don't keep firearms in this house.

34. Has anybody seen the sideburns trimmer?

33. You can't feed that to the dog.

32. I thought Graceland was tacky.

31. No kids in the back of the pickup, it's just not safe.

30. Wrasslin's fake.

29. Honey, did you mail that donation to Greenpeace.

28. We're vegetarians.

27. Do you think my gut is too big?

26. I'll have grapefruit and grapes instead of biscuits and gravy.

25. Honey, we don't need another dog.

24. Who's Richard Petty?

23. Give me the small bag of pork rinds.

22. Too many deer heads detract from the dÈcor.

21. Spittin' is such a nasty habit.

20. I just couldn't find a thing at Wal-mart today.

19. Trim the fat off that steak.

18. Cappuccino tastes better than espresso.

17. The tires on that truck are too big.

16. I'll have the arugula and radicchio salad.

15. I've got it all on the C drive.

14. Unsweetened tea tastes better.

13. Would you like your salmon poached or broiled?

12. My fiancé, Bobbie Jo, is registered at Tiffany's.

11. I've got two cases of Zima for the Super Bowl.

10. Little Debbie snack cakes have too many fat grams.

9. Checkmate.

8. She's too young to be wearing a bikini.

7. Does the salad bar have bean sprouts?

6. Hey, here's an episode of "Hee Haw" that we haven't seen.

5. I don' have a favorite college team.

4. Be sure to bring my salad dressing on the side.

3. I believe you cooked those green beans too long.

2. Those shorts ought to be a little longer, Darla

AND

#1. Nope, no more for me. I'm drivin' tonight.

"A Short Lesson On "Southernisms"

If you are from the northern states and planning on visiting or moving to the South, there are a few things you should know that will help you adapt to the difference in lifestyles:

The North has sun-dried toe-mah-toes,
The south has 'mater samiches.

The North has coffee houses,
The South has Waffle Houses.

The North has switchblade knives,
The South has Lee Press on Nails.

The North has double last names,
The south has double first names.

The North has Ted Kennedy,
The South has Jesse Helms.
The North has an ambulance,
The South has an amalance.

The North has the Mafia,
The South has the Klan.
The North has Indy car races,
The South has stock car races.

The North has Cream of Wheat,
The South has grits.

The North has green salads,
The South has collard greens.

The North has lobsters,
The South has craw dads.

The North has the rust belt,
The South has the Bible Belt.

If you run your car into a ditch, don't panic. Four men in a four-wheel drive pickup truck with a tow chain will be along shortly. Don't try to help them, just stay out of their way. This is what they live for.

Don't be surprised to find movie rentals and bait in the same store. Don't buy food at this store!

You Are a True Redneck . . .
    If you have a complete set of salad bowls and they all say Cool Whip on the side,

    If the biggest city you've ever been to is Wal-Mart,

    If your working T.V. sits on top of your non-working T.V.,

If you thought the Unabomber was a wrestler,

If you've ever used your ironing board as a buffet table,

If you think a quarter horse is that ride in front of K-Mart,

If your neighbors think you're a detective because a cop always brings you home,

If a tornado hits your neighborhood and does $100,000 worth of improvements,

If you've ever used a toilet brush as a back scratcher,

If you missed 5th grade graduation because you had jury duty,

If you think fast food is hitting a deer at 65mph,

If somebody tells you that you've got something in your teeth and you take your teeth out to see what it is.

And, You Might Be a Yankee ...

If you think barbeque is a verb meaning "to cook outside",

If you think Heinz Ketchup is SPICY!,

If you don't have any problems pronouncing "Worcestershire Sauce" correctly,

If for breakfast, you would prefer potatoes au gratin to grits,

If you don't know what a "Moon Pie" is,

If you've never had a grain alcohol,

If you've never, ever eaten okra,

If you eat fried chicken with a knife and fork,

If you've never seen a live chicken, and the only cows you've seen are on road trips,

If you have no idea what a polecat is,

If you don't see anything wrong with putting a sweater on a poodle,

If you don't have bangs,

If you would rather vacation at Martha's Vineyard than at Six Flags,

If more than two generations of your family have been kicked out of the same prep school in Connecticut,

If you would rather have your son become a lawyer than grow up to get his own TV fishing show,

If instead of referring to two or more people as "y'all," you call them "you guys," even if both of them are women,

If you don't think Howard Stern has an accent,

If you have never planned your summer vacation around a gun-and-knife show,

If you think more money should go to important scientific research at your university than to pay the salary of the head football coach,

If you don't have at least one can of WD-40 somewhere around the house,

If the last time you smiled was when you prevented someone from getting on an on-ramp on the highway,

If you don't have any hats in your closet that advertise a feed store.

If the farthest south you've ever been is the perfume counter at Neiman Marcus,

If you call binoculars "opera glasses",

AND if you can't spit out the car window without pulling over to the side of the road and stopping!

David C. Powell, M.D.

REDNECK DRIVERS LICENSE:
Plez complete this paper, best ya can.

Last name: _____

First name:

☐	Billy-Bob	☐	Bobby-Sue
☐	Billy-Joe	☐	Bobby-Jo
☐	Billy-Ray	☐	Bobby-Ann
☐	Billy-Sue	☐	Bobby-Lee
☐	Billy-Mae	☐	Bobby-Ellen
☐	Billy-Jack	☐	Bobby-Beth Ann Sue

Age: _____(If unsure, guess)

Sex: ☐ M ☐ F ☐ None

Sue Size: _____ Left _____Right

Occupation:

☐	Farmer	☐	Mechanic
☐	Hair Dresser	☐	Waitress
☐	Un-employed	☐	Dirty Politician

Spouse's Name: _____

2nd Spouse's Name: _____

3rd Spouse's Name: _____

Lover's Name: _____

2nd Lover's Name: _____

Relationship with Spouse:

☐	Sister	☐	Aunt
☐	Brother	☐	Uncle
☐	Mother	☐	Son
☐	Father	☐	Daughter
☐	Cousin	☐	Pet

Number of children living in household? _____

Number of children living in shed? _____

Number of children that are yours? _____

Mother's Name:_____

Father's Name:_____

Education: 1 2 3 4 (Circle highest grade completed)

If you obtained a higher education, what was your major?

☐ 5th Grade   ☐ 6th grade

Do you ☐ own or ☐ rent your mobile home?

Vehicles you own and where you keep them:

_____Total number of vehicles you own

_____Number of vehicles that still crank

_____Number of vehicles in front yard

_____Number of vehicles in back yard

_____Number of vehicles on cement blocks

(If over 10, are you still learnin'?   ☐Yes   ☐ No)

Firearms you own and where you keep them:

_____truck   _____kitchen

_____bedroom   _____bathroom / outhouse

_____shed   _____Pawnshop

Model and year of your pickup: _____ 194_____

Do you have a gun rack?

☐ Yes   ☐ No; If no, please explain:

Newspapers/magazines you subscribe to:

☐ The National Enquirer   ☐ The Globe
☐ TV Guide   ☐ Soap Opera Digest
☐ Rifle and Shotgun   ☐ Bassmasters

_____Number of times you've seen a UFO
_____Number of times you've seen Elvis
_____Number of times you've seen Elvis in a UFO

How often do you bathe: ☐ Weekly ☐ Monthly
☐ Not applicable

How many teeth in YOUR mouth? _____
Color of teeth: ☐ Yellow ☐ Brown ☐ Brownish-Yellow
☐ Black ☐ N/A

Brand of chewing tobacco you prefer: ☐ Red-Man ☐ Skoal

How far is your home from a paved road?

☐ 1 mile ☐ 2 miles ☐ don't know

- Redneck Driving Etiquette -

Dim your headlights for approaching vehicles, even if the gun is loaded and the deer is in sight.

When approaching a four-way stop, the vehicle with the largest tires always has the right of way.

Never tow another car using pantyhose and duct tape.

When sending your wife down the road with a gas can, it is impolite to ask her to bring back beer.

Never relieve yourself from a moving vehicle, especially when driving.

Do not remove the seats from the car so that all your kids can fit in.

Do not lay rubber while traveling in a funeral procession.

- Redneck Personal Hygiene -

Unlike clothes and shoes, a toothbrush should never be a hand-me-down item.

If you have to vacuum the bed, it's time to change the sheets.

While ears need to be cleaned regularly, this is a job that should be done in private using one's OWN truck keys.

Plucking unwanted nose hair is time-consuming work. A cigarette lighter and a small tolerance for pain can accomplish the same goal and save hours.

Note: It's a good idea to keep a bucket of water handy when using this method.

- Redneck Dining Out -

Remember to leave a generous tip for good service. After all, their mobile home costs just as much as yours.

- Redneck Entertaining in Your Home –

A centerpiece for the table should never be anything prepared by a taxidermist.

Do not allow the dog to eat at the table ... no matter how good his manners are.

Always offer to bait your date's hook, especially on the first date.

- Redneck Theater Etiquette –

Crying babies should be taken to the lobby and picked up immediately after the movie has ended.

Refrain from talking to characters on the screen. Tests have proven they can't hear you.

- Redneck Wedding Etiquette –

Livestock is usually a poor choice for a wedding gift.

It's not okay for the groom to bring a date to a wedding.

A bridal veil made of window screen is not only cost effective, but also a proven fly deterrent.

For the groom, at least rent a tux. A leisure suit with a cummerbund and a clean bowling shirt can create a natty appearance. Though uncomfortable, say yes to socks and shoes for this special occasion.

- Redneck Etiquette for All Occasions –

Never take a beer to a job interview or ask if they press charges.

Always identify people in your yard before shooting at them.
Always say "Excuse me" after getting sick in someone else's car.

It's considered tacky to take a cooler to church.

Even if you're certain that you are included in the will, it's considered tacky to drive a U-Haul to the funeral home.

Always provide an alibi to the policy for family members.

"True Southerners"

Only A true Southerner know the difference between a hissie fit and a conniption and that you don't "have" them, but you "pitch" them.

Nobody but a true Southerner knows how many fish, collard greens, turnip greens, peas, beans, etc. make a "mess".

A true Southerner can show or point out to you the general direction of "yonder."

A true Southerner knows exactly how long "directly" is — as in "Going to town, be back directly."

Even true southern babies know that "Gimme some sugar" is not a request for the white, granular sweet substance that sits in a pretty little bowl in the middle of the table.

All true Southerners know exactly when "by and by" is. They might not use the term, but they know the concept well.

True Southerners know instinctively that the best gesture of solace for a neighbor who's got trouble is a plate of hot fried chicken and big bowl of cold potato salad. (If the trouble is a real crisis, they also know to add a large banana puddin'.)

True Southerners grow up knowing the difference between "right near" and "a right far piece." They know that "just down the road, can be 1 mile or 20 miles.

True Southerners both know and understand the differences between redneck, a good ol' boy, and po' white trash.

No true Southerner would ever assume that the car with the flashing turn signal is actually going to make a turn.

True Southerners know that "fixin" can be used both as a noun, verb, and adverb.

A true Southerner knows how to understand Southern: a booger can be a resident of the nose, a descriptive ("That ol' booger!") or something that jumps out at you in the dark and scares you sense-less.

True Southerners make friends standing in lines. We don't do "queues," we do "lines." And when we're in line, we talk to every-body.

Put 100 southerners in a room and half of them will discover they're related, if only by marriage.

True Southerners never refer to one person as "ya'll"

True Southerners know grits come from corn and how to eat them.

Every true Southerner knows tomatoes with eggs, bacon, grits and coffee are perfectly wonderful; that red-eye gravy is also a breakfast food; that fried green tomatoes are not breakfast food.

When you hear someone say, "Well, I called myself lookin', you know you're in the presence of a genuine Southerner.

Southerners say "sweet tea" and "sweet milk." Sweet tea indicates the need for sugar and lots of it – we do not like our tea unsweet-ened; "sweet milk" means you don't want buttermilk.

And a true Southerner knows you don't scream obscenities at little old ladies who drive 30mph on the freeway – you say, "Bless her heart" and go on your way.

Redneck Behavior ? ? ? ? ? ? ? ? ?

- Any of your children were conceived in a car wash.

- You take your dog for a walk and you both use the same tree to relieve yourselves.

- The most common phrase heard in your house is, "Somebody go jiggle the handle."

- You've ever been kicked out of the zoo for heckling the monkeys.

- Your kids take a siphon hose to "Show and Tell."

- You pick your teeth from a catalog.

- You can entertain yourself for more than an hour with a fly swatter.

- You've ever stolen toilet paper.

- Your property has been mistaken for a recycling center.

- You've ever plucked a nose hair with a pair of pliers.

- There's an expired license plate hanging on your living room wall.

- Your toilet paper has page numbers on it.

- You've ever been pumping gas and another customer asks you to check his oil.

- You think the Bud Bowl is real.

- You consider dating second cousins as "Playing the field".

- You think "six to ten pounds" on the side of the Pampers box means how much the diaper will hold.

- You paint your car with house paint.

- You can drink beer through your nose.

- Your dog goes "oink!"

- You think the Nutcracker is something you did off the hive dive.

- Your mailbox is made out of old auto parts.

- You know how to milk a goat.

- You have a black eye and a hickey at the same time.

- Your kids have a three-day old Kool-Aid mustache.

- Your TV gets 512 channels, but you go outside to use the bathroom.

- You offer to give somebody the shirt off your back and they don't want it.

- You think toilet water is good for drinking.

- Your chili's secret ingredient comes from the bait shop.

- Turning on your lights involves pulling a string.

- You wore curlers to your wedding so you would look nice at the reception.

Chapter X

Christmas, or Ho, Ho, Ho - - -

David C. Powell, M.D.

"Santa" Memo

I have been watching you very closely to see if you have been good this year and since you have, I will be telling my elves to make some goodies for me to leave under your tree at Christmas. I was going to bring you all gifts from the "12 days of Christmas", but we had a little problem. The 12 fiddlers fiddling have all come down with VD from fiddling with the 10 ladies dancing, the 11 lords leaping have knocked up the 8 maids a-milking, and the 9 pipers piping have been arrested for doing weird things to the 7 swans a-swimming. The 6 geese a-laying, 4 calling birds, 3 French hens, 2 turtle doves and the partridge in a pear tree have me up to my sled runner in bird shit.

On top of all this, Mrs. Claus is going through menopause, 8 of my reindeer are in heat, the elves have joined the gay liberation and some people who can't read a calendar have scheduled Christmas for the 5th of January.

Maybe next year I will be able to get my shit together and bring you the things you want. This year I suggest you get your asses down to Wal-Mart before everything is gone.

Sincerely,

Santa Claus

12 Days of Christmas "Trivia"

There is one Christmas Carol that has always baffled me. What in the world do leaping lords, French hens, swimming swans, and especially the partridge who won't come out of the pear tree have to do with Christmas? Well just read on:

From 1558 until 1829, Roman Catholics in England were not permitted to practice their faith openly. Someone during that era wrote this carol as a catechism song for the young Catholics. It has two levels of meaning, the surface meaning plus a hidden meaning known only to members of their church.

Each element in the carol has a code word for a religious reality which the children could remember:

1) The partridge in a pear tree was Jesus Christ.

2) Two turtle doves were the Old and New Testaments.

3) Three French hens stood for faith, hope, and love.

4) The four calling birds were the four gospels of Matthew, Mark, Luke and John.

5) The five golden rings recalled the Torah or Law, the first five books.

6) The six geese a-laying stood for the six days of creating.

7) Seven swans a-swimming represented the sevenfold gifts of the Holy Spirit – Prophesy,

Serving, Teaching, Exhortation, Contribution, Leadership, and Mercy.

8) The eight maids a-milking were the eight beatitudes.

9) Nine ladies dancing were the nine fruits of the Holy Spirit — Love, Joy, Peace, Patience, Kindness, Goodness, Faithfulness, Gentleness, and Self Control.

10) The ten lords a leaping were the ten commandments.

11) The eleven pipers piping stood for the eleven faithful disciples.

12) The twelve drummers drumming symbolized the twelve points of belief in the Apostles Creed.

****

"Antlers" !

According to the Alaska Department of fish and game, while both male and female reindeer grow antlers in the summer each year, male reindeer drop their antlers at the beginning of winter, usually late November to mid-December.

Female reindeer retain their antlers 'til after they give birth in the spring. Therefore, according to the historical rendition depicting Santa's reindeer, every single one of them, from Rudolph to Blitzen had to be a female.

We should have known. Only women would be able to drag a fat man in a red velvet suit all around the world in one night and not get lost!

"Martha Stewart's Holiday Calendar"

December 1   Blanch carcass from Thanksgiving turkey. Spray paint gold; turn upside down and use as a sleigh to hold Christmas cards.

December 2   Have Mormon Tabernacle Choir record outgoing Christmas message for answering machine.

December 3   Using candlewick and handgilded miniature pine cones, fashion cat-o-nine-tails. Flog Gardener.

December 4   Repaint Sistine Chapel ceiling in ecru, with mocha trim.

December 5   Get new eyeglasses. Grind lenses myself.

December 6   Fax family Christmas newsletter to Pulitzer committee for consideration.

December 7   Debug windows '95.

December 10   Align carpets to adjust for curvature of Earth.

December 11   Lay Faberge egg.

December 12   Take Dog apart. Disinfect. Reassemble.

December 13   Collect Dentures. They make excellent pastry cutters, particularly for decorative pie crusts.

December 14   Install plumbing in gingerbread house.

December 15   Replace air in mini-van tires with Glade "holiday scents" in case tires are shot out at the mall.

December 17   Child proof the Christmas tree with garland of razor wire.

December 19   Adjust legs of chairs so each Christmas dinner guest will be same height when sitting at this or her assigned seat.

December 20   Dip sheep and cows in egg whites and roll in confectioner's sugar to add a festive sparkle to the pasture.

December 21   Drain city reservoir; refill with mulled cider, orange slices and cinnamon sticks.

December 22   Float votive candles in toilet tank.

December 23   Seed clouds for white Christmas.

December 24   Do my annual good deed. Go to several stores. Be seen engaged in last minutes Christmas shopping, thus making many people feel less inadequate than they really are.

December 25   Bear son. Swaddle. Lay in color coordinated manger scented with homemade potpourri.

December 26   Organize spice racks by genus and phylum.

December 27   Build snowman in exact likeness of God.

December 31   New Year's Eve! Give staff their resolutions. Call a friend in each time zone of the world as the clock strikes midnight in that country.

? ? ? ? ? ? ? "T'was the Night Before Christmas" ? ? ? ? ? ? ? ?

T'was the Night Before Christmas – Old Santa was pissed
He cussed out the elves and threw down his list
Miserable little brats, ungrateful little jerks
I have a good mind to scrap the whole works.

I've busted my ass for damn near a year
Instead of "thanks Santa" – what do I hear
The old lady bitches cause I work late at night

I Need a Copy of That

The elves want more money – the reindeer all fight.

Rudolph got drunk and goosed all the maids
Donner is pregnant and Vixen has AIDS
And just when I thought that things would get better
Those assholes from IRS sent me a letter.

They say I owe taxes – if that ain't damn funny
Who the hell ever sent Santa Clause any money
And the kids these days – they all are the pits
They want the impossible . . . those mean little shits.

I spent a whole year making wagons and sleds
Assembling dolls....their arms legs and heads
I made a ton of yo-yo's – no request for them
They want computers and robots...they think I'm IBM!

If you think they're bad... just picture this
Try holding those brats... with their pants full of piss
They pull on my nose – they grab at my beard
And if I don't smile.. the parents think I'm weird.

Flying through the air... dodging the trees
Falling down chimneys and skinning my knees
I'm quitting this job...there's just no enjoyment
I'll sit on my fat ass and draw unemployment
There's no Christmas this year ...now you know the rea-
son
I found me a blonde..I'm going SOUTH for the season ! !

&%/&%/*&%/*&^%/*&%/*&%/*&%/*&%/*&%/*&%/*&%/*&%/*&%/*&%/*&%/*&%/*&%/*

David C. Powell, M.D.

The "Politically Correct" Days of Christmas …."

On the 12th day of the Euro centrically imposed midwinter festival, my Significant Other in a consenting adult, monogamous relationship gave to me:

TWELVE males reclaiming their inner warrior through ritual drumming,

ELEVEN pipers piping (plus the 18-member pit orchestra made up of members in good standing of the Musicians Equity Union as called for in their union contract even though they will not be asked to play a note),

TEN melanin deprived testosterone-poisoned scions of the patriarchal ruling class system leaping,

NINE persons engaged in rhythmic self-expression,

EIGHT economically disadvantaged female persons stealing milk-products from enslaved Bovine-Americans,

SEVEN endangered swans swimming on federally protected wetlands,

SIX enslaved Fowl-American producing stolen non-human animal products,

FIVE golden symbols of culturally sanctioned enforced domestic incarceration,

(NOTE: after members of the Animal Liberation Front threatened to throw red paint at my computer, the calling birds, French hens and partridge have been reintroduced to their native habitat. To avoid further Animal-American enslavement, the remaining gift package has been revised.)

FOUR hours of recorded whale songs,

THREE deconstructionist poets,

TWO Sierra Club calendars printed on recycled processed tree carcasses,

AND

ONE Spotted Owl activist chained to an old-growth pear tree.

<u>Merry Christmas.</u>   <u>Happy Chanukah.</u>   <u>Good Kwanzaa.</u>
<u>Blessed Yule.</u>

Oh, heck! Unless, of course, you are suffering from Seasonally Affected Disorder (SAD). If this be the case, please substitute this gratuitous call for celebration with suggestion that you have a thoroughly adequate day!

&%&%*&%*&^%*&%*&%*&%*&%*&%*&%*&%*&%*&%*&%*&%*&%*&%*

And, File this in the Bah Humbug Folder !

Effective immediately, the following economizing measures are being implemented in the "Twelve Days of Christmas" subsidiary:

1) The partridge will be retained, but the pear tree, which never produced the cash crop forecasted, will be replaced by a plastic hanging plant, providing considerable savings In maintenance;

2) Two turtle doves represent a redundancy that is simply not cost effective. In addition, their romance during working hours could not be condoned. The positions are, therefore, eliminated;

3) The three French hens will remain intact. After all, everyone loves the French;

4) The four calling birds will be replaced by an automated voice mail system, with a call waiting option. An analysis is underway to determine who the birds have been calling, how often and how long they talked;

5) The five golden rings have been put on hold by the Board of Directors. Maintaining a portfolio based on one commodity

could have negative implications for institutional investors. Diversification into other precious metals, as well as a mix of T-Bills and high technology stocks, appear to be in order;

6) The six geese-a-laying constitutes a luxury which can no longer be afforded. It has long been felt that the production rate of one egg per goose per day was an example of the general decline in productivity. Three geese will be let go, and an upgrading in the selection procedure by personnel will assure management that, from now on, every goose it gets will be a good one;

7) The seven swans-a-swimming is obviously a number chosen in better times. The function is primarily decorative. Mechanical swans are on order. The current swans will be retrained to learn some new strokes thereby enhancing their outplacement;

8) As you know, the eight maids-a-milking concept has been under heavy scrutiny by the EEOC. A male/female balance in the workforce is being sought. The more militant maids consider this a dead-end job with no upward mobility. Automation of the process may permit the maids to try a-mending, a-mentoring, or a-mulching;

9) Nine ladies dancing has always been an odd number. This function will be phased out as these individuals grow older and can no longer do the steps,

10) Ten Lords-a-leaping is overkill. The high cost of Lords, plus the expense of international air travel, prompted the Compensation Committee to suggest replacing this group with ten out-of-work congressmen. While leaping ability may be somewhat sacrificed, the savings are significant as we expect an oversupply of unemployed congressmen this year;

11) Eleven pipers piping and twelve drummers drumming is a simple case of the band getting too big. A substitution with a string quartet, a cutback on new music, and no uniforms, will produce savings which will drop right to the bottom line;

Overall, we can expect a substantial reduction in assorted people, fowl, animals and related expenses. Though incomplete, studies indicate that stretching deliveries over twelve days is inefficient. If we can drop ship in one day, service levels will be improved.

Regarding the lawsuit filed by the attorney's association seeking expansion to include the legal profession ("thirteen lawyers-a-suing"), a decision is pending.

Deeper cuts may be necessary in the future to remain competitive. Should that happen, the Board will request management to scrutinize the Snow White Division to see if seven dwarves is the right number.

Letter from Santa :

I regret to inform you that, effective immediately, I will no longer be able to serve Southern United States on Christmas Eve. Due to the overwhelming current population of the earth, my contract was re-negotiated by North American Fairies and Elves Local 209.

I now serve only certain areas of Ohio, Indiana, Illinois, Wisconsin, and Michigan. As part of the new and better contract, I also get longer breaks for milk and cookies, so keep that in mind.

However, I'm certain that your children will be in good hands with your local replacement who happens to be my third cousin, Bubba Claus.

His side of the family is from the South Pole. He shares my goal of delivering toys to all the good boys and girls; however, there are a few differences between us. (Differences such as:

1) There is no danger of a Grinch stealing your presents from Bubba Claus. He has a gun rack on his sleigh and a bumper sticker that reads:"These toys insured by Smith and Wesson."

2) Instead of milk and cookies, Bubby Claus prefers that children leave an RC Cola and pork rinds (or a Moon Pie) on the fireplace. And Bubba doesn't smoke a pipe. He dips a little snuff though, so please have an empty spit can handy.

3) Bubba Claus' sleigh is pulled by floppy-eared, flyin' coon dogs instead of reindeer. I made the mistake of loaning him a couple of my reindeer one time, and Blitzen's head now overlooks Bubba's fireplace.

4) You won't hear "On Comet, on Cupid, on Donner and Blitzen,....." when Bubba Claus arrives. Instead, you'll hear, "On Earnhardt, on Wallace, on Martin and Labonte. On Ruddy, on Jarrett, on Elliott and Petty."

5) "Ho, ho ho!" has been replaced by "Yee Haw!" And you also are likely to hear Bubba's elves respond, "I her'd dat!"

6) As required by Southern highway laws, Bubba Claus' sleigh does have a Yosemite Sam Safety triangle on the back with the words "Back Off". The last I heard it also had other decorations on the sleigh back as well. One is a Ford or Chevy logo with lights that race through the letters and the other is a caricature of me (Santa Claus) going wee wee on the Tooth Fairy.

7) The usual Christmas movie classics such as "Miracle on 34th Street" and "It's a Wonderful Life" will not be shown in your negotiated viewing area. Instead, you'll see "Boss Hogg Saves

Christmas" and "Smokey and the Bandit IV" featuring Burt Reynolds as Bubba Claus and dozens of state patrol cars crashing into each other.

8) Bubba Claus doesn't wear a belt. If I were you, I'd make sure you, the wife, and the kids turn the other way when he bends over to put presents under the tree.

9) And finally, lovely Christmas songs have been sung about me like "Rudolph The Red-nosed Reindeer" and Bing Crosby's "Santa Claus Is coming to town." This year songs about Bubba Claus will be played on all the AM radio stations in the South. Those song titles will be Mark Chesnutt's "Bubba Claus Shot the Jukebox" and "Grandma got Run'd Over by a Reindeer."

Sincerely Yours,

Santa Claus
Member of North American Fairies and Elves Local 209

Jingle Gates"

'Twas the night before Christmas, when all through the house,
Not a creature was stirring, except Papa's mouse.
The computer was humming, the icons were hopping,
As Papa did last-minute Internet shopping.
The stockings were hung by the modem with care
In hope that St. Nicholas would bring new software.
The children were nestled all snug in their beds,
While visions of computer games danced in their heads.

Dark Forces for Billy, and Doom II for Dan,

And Carmen Sandiego for Pamela Ann.
The letters to Santa had been sent out by Mom,
To
santaclaus@toyshop.northpole.com

Which has now been re-routed to Washington State
Because Santa's workshop has been bought by Bill Gates.
All the elves and reindeer have had to skedaddle
To flashy new quarters in suburban Seattle.

After centuries of a life that was simple and spare,
St. Nicholas is suddenly a new billionaire,
With a shiny red Porsche in the place of his sleigh,
And a house on Lake Washington that's just down the way
From where Bill has his mansion.

The old fellow preens in black Gucci boots
And red Calvin Klein jeans.
The elves have stock options and desks with a view,
Where they write computer code for Johnny and Sue.

No more dolls or toy soldiers or little toy drums
(Ahem – pardon me)
No more dolls or tin soldiers or little toy drums
Will be under the tree, only campact disk ROMS
With the Microsoft label, you see.
So spin up your drive,
From now on Christmas runs only on Windows 95.

More rapid than eagles
The competitors came,
And Bill whistled, and shouted,
And called them by name.
"Now, ADOBE! Now CLARIS! Now, INTUIT! Too,
Now, APPLE! And NETSCAPE!
You all are through!

It's Microsoft's SANTA that the kids can't resist,
It's the ultimate software with a traditional twist.

Get 'em young, keep 'em long, is Microsoft's scheme,
And a merger with Santa is a marketer's dream.

To the top of the NASDAQ! To the top of the DOW!
Now dash away! Dash away! Dash away – WOW!

And Mama in her 'kerchief and I in my cap,
Had just settled down for a long winter's nap.

When out on the lawn there arose such a clatter,
The whirr and the hum of our satellite platter.

As it turned toward that new Christmas star in the sky,
The SANTALITE owned by the Microsoft guy.

As I sprang from my bed and was turning around,
My computer turned on with a Jingle-Bells sound.

And there on the screen was smiling Bill Gates
Next to jolly old Santa, two arm-in-arm mates.

And I heard them exclaim in voices so bright,
Have a MICROSOFT CHRISTMAS,
And to all a GOOD NIGHT.

Chapter XI

MEN vs. WOMEN

"Two Warring Tribes That Call"
A
"Truce to Mate..."

HORMONE HOSTAGE:

The *Hormone Hostage* knows that there are days in the month when all a man has to do is open his mouth and he takes his life in his own hands! This is a handy guide that should be as common as a driver's license in the wallet of every husband, boyfriend, or significant other!

DANGEROUS: What's for dinner?

SAFER: Can I help you with dinner?

SAFEST: Where would you like to go for dinner?

DANGEROUS: Are you wearing that?

SAFER: Gee, you look good in brown.

SAFEST: WOW! Look at you!

DANGEROUS: What are you so worked up about?

SAFER: Could we be over-reacting?

SAFEST: Here's fifty dollars.

DANGEROUS: Should you be eating that?

SAFER: You know, there are a lot of apples left.

SAFEST: Can I get you a glass of wine with that?

DANGEROUS: What did you do all day?

SAFER: I hope you didn't over do it today.

SAFEST: I've always loved you in that robe!

How to Impress A Woman: How to Impress A Man:

How to Impress A Woman:	How to Impress A Man:
☺ Wine her,	
☺ Dine her,	
☺ Call her,	
☺ Hug her,	
☺ Support her,	
☺ Hold her,	1) Show up naked...,
☺ Surprise her,	
☺ Compliment her,	
☺ Smile at her,	
☺ Listen to her,	
☺ Laugh with her,	
☺ Cry with her,	
☺ Romance her,	2) Bring food...,
☺ Encourage her,	
☺ Believe in her,	
☺ Pray with her,	
☺ Pray for her,	
☺ Cuddle with her,	
☺ Shop with her,	
☺ Give her jewelry,	3) Don't block the TV.
☺ Buy her flowers,	
☺ Hold her hand,	
☺ Write love letters to her,	
☺ Go to the end of the Earth and back again for her.	

So God asked Adam, "What is wrong with you?"

Adam said, "I don't have anybody to talk to."

God said He was going to make Adam a companion and that it would be a woman. God said, "this person will gather food for you, cook for you, and when you discover clothing, she'll wash it for you. She will always agree with every decision you make. She will bear your children and never ask you to get up in the middle of the night to take care of them. She will not nag you and will always be the first to admit that she was wrong when you've had a disagreement. She will never have a headache and will freely give you love and passion whenever you need it."

Adam asked God, "What will a woman like that cost?" God replied, "An arm and a leg."

Then Adam asked, "What can I get for a rib?"

OLDIES BUT GOODIES ! ! !

What's the best form of birth control after 50? Nudity

What's the difference between a girlfriend and a wife? 45 pounds

What's the difference between a boyfriend and a husband? 45 minutes.

How many women does it take to change a light bulb?
None , they just sit there in the dark and bitch.

What's the fastest way to a man's heart? Through his chest with a sharp knife.

Why do men want to marry virgins? They can't stand criticism.

I Need a Copy of That

Why is it so hard for women to find men that are sensitive, caring and good looking?
Because those men already have boyfriends.

What's the difference between a new husband and a new dog?
After a year the dog is still excited to see you.

What makes men chase women they have no intention of marrying?
The same urges that makes dogs chase cars they have no intention of driving.

What do you call a smart blond? A golden retriever.

Why does a bride always wear white? Because it's good for the dishwasher to match the stove and refrigerator.

A brunette, a blonde, and a red-head are all in the third grade; who has the biggest boobs?
The blonde because she's 18.

What's the quickest way to clear out a men's room? Say, "nice dick".

Why don't bunnies make noise when they have sex? Because they have cotton balls.

What's the difference between a porcupine and a BMW?
A porcupine has the pricks on the outside.

What did the blonde say when she found out she was pregnant?
"Are you sure it's mine?"

What's the difference between beer nuts and deer nuts?
Beer nuts are $1.00 and deer nuts are always under a buck.

If you are having sex with two women and one more walks in, what do you have?
Divorce proceedings, most likely.

Why did OJ Simpson want to move to West Virginia? Everyone has the same DNA.

Why do men find it difficult to make eye contact? Breasts don't have eyes.

How do you get a sweet little 80-year-old lady to say f_ _k?
Get another sweet little 80-year-old lady to yell "BINGO".

IT'S A PLAN - THINK ABOUT IT!

Take all American women who are within five years of menopause — train us for a few weeks, outfit us with automatic weapons, grenades, gas masks, moisturizer with SPF15, Prozac, hormones, chocolate, and canned tuna — drop us (parachuted, preferably) across the landscape of Afghanistan, and let us do what comes naturally.

Think about it. Our anger quotient alone, even when doing standard stuff like grocery shopping and paying bills, is formidable enough to make even armed men in turbans tremble.

We've had our children, we would gladly suffer or die to protect them and their future. We'd like to get away from our husbands, if they haven't left already. And for those of us who are single, the prospect of finding a good man with whom to share life is about as likely as being struck by lightening.

We have nothing to lose.

We've survived the water diet, the protein diet, the carbohydrate diet, and the grapefruit diet in gyms and saunas across America and never lost a pound. We can easily survive months in the hostile terrain of Afghanistan with no food at all!

We've spent years tracking down our husband or lovers in bars, hardware stores, or sporting events ... finding Bin Laden in some cave will be no problem.

Uniting all the warring tribes of Afghanistan in a new government? Oh, please ... we've planned the seating arrangements for in-laws and extended families at Thanksgiving dinners for years ... we understand tribal warfare.

Between us, we've divorced enough husbands to know every trick there is for how they hide, launder, or cover up bank accounts and money sources. We know how to find that money and we know how to seize it ... with or without the government's help!

Let us go and fight. The Taliban hates women. Imagine their terror as we crawl like ants, with hot-flashes, over their godforsaken terrain.

I'm going to write my Congresswoman, *you should, too!*

How to Shower Like A Woman ....

- Take off clothing and place it in a sectioned laundry hamper according to lights, darks, whites, manmade or natural.

- Walk to the bathroom wearing long dressing gown.

- If husband seen along the way, cover up any exposed flesh and rush to the bathroom.

- Look at womanly physique in the mirror and stick out belly.

- Complain and whine about getting fat.

- Get in shower.

- Look for facecloth, arm cloth, loin cloth, long loofah, wide loofah, and pumice stone.

- Wash hair once with Cucumber and Lamphrey shampoo with 83 added vitamins.

- Wash hair again with Cucumber and Lamphrey shampoo with 83 added vitamins.

- Condition hair with cucumber and Lamphrey conditioner with enhanced natural crocus oil.

- Leave on hair for 15 minutes.

- Wash face with crushed apricot facial scrub for ten minutes until red and raw.

- Wash entire rest of body with Ginger Nut and Jaffa Cake body wash.

- Rinse conditioner off hair taking at least 15 minutes to make sure that it's all come off.

- Shave armpits and legs.

- Consider shaving bikini area but decide to get it waxed instead.

- Scream loudly when husband flushes toilet and water loses pressure and turns red hot.

- Turn off shower.

- Squeegee all wet surfaces in shower. Spray mold spots with Tilex.

- Get out of shower. Dry with towel the size of a small African country.

- Wrap hair in super absorbent second towel.

- Check entire body for remotest sign of spots. Attack with nails / tweezers (if you can find them).

- Return to bedroom wearing long dressing gown and towel on head.

- If husband seen, cover up any exposed areas and then rush to bedroom to spend hour and half getting dressed.

How to Shower Like a Man . . . .

- Take off clothes while sitting on bed and leave them in a pile.

- Walk naked to the bathroom.

- If wife seen, shake kn*b at her while shouting WayHey !!

- Look in mirror and suck in gut to see your manly physique.

- Admire size of kn*b in mirror, scratch b*llocks and smell fingers for one last whiff.

- Get in shower. Don't bother to look for wash cloth – don't need one.

- Wash face.

- Wash armpits.

- Laugh at how loud farts sound in the shower.

- Wash b*llock and the surrounding area.

- Wash a*se, leaving hair on soap.

- Shampoo hair but do not use conditioner. Make Mohican hairstyle with shampoo.

- Pull back curtain to see self in mirror. P*ss in shower.

- Rinse off and get out of shower.

- Fail to notice water on floor because shower curtain outside tub for whole shower time.

- Partially dry off. Look at self in mirror, flex muscles and admire size of kn*b again.

- Leave shower curtain open and wet bath mat on floor.

- Leave bathroom light and fan on.

- Return to bedroom with towel around waist.

- If you pass wife, pull off towel, grab kn*b, go "Yeah baby" and thrust pelvis at her.

- Put on yesterdays clothes.

IT'S GREAT TO BE A MAN:

1) Your rear-end is never a factor in a job interview.

2) Your orgasms are real. Always.

3) Your last name stays put.

4) You never feel compelled to stop a friend from getting laid.

5) Hot wax never comes near your public area.

6) The garage is all yours.

7) Wedding plans take care of themselves.

8) Chocolate is just another snack.

9) You can be president.

10) You can wear a white T-shirt to a water park.

11) Car mechanics tell you the truth.

12) You don't give a rats ass if someone notices your new haircut.

13) If you retain water, it's in a canteen.

14) Porn movies are designed with you in mind.

15) You can open all your own jars.

16) You never have to drive to another gas station because this one is just too icky.

17) Same work ... more pay.

18) Wrinkles add character.

19) Wedding Dress $5000; Tux rental $100.

20) People never stare at your chest when you're talking to them.

21) New shoes don't cut, blister, or mangle your feet.

22) One mood, ALL the damn time.

23) Phone conversations are over in 30 seconds flat.

24) A five-day vacation requires only one suitcase.

25) You can leave the motel bed unmade.

26) You can kill your own food.

27) If someone forgets to invite you to something, he or she can still be your friend.

28) Your underwear is $8.95 for a three-pack.

29) You can quietly enjoy a car ride from the passenger seat.

30) Three pairs of shoes are more than enough.

31) You can quietly watch a game with your buddy for hours without ever thinking: "He must be made at me."

32) You can drop by to see a friend without having to bring a little gift.

33) If another guy shows up at the party in the same outfit, you just might become lifelong friends.

34) You are not expected to know the names of more than five colors.

35) You don't have to stop and think of which way to turn a nut on a bolt.

36) You almost never have strap problems in public.

37) You are unable to see wrinkles in your clothes.

38) The same hairstyle lasts for years, maybe decades.

39) You don't have to shave below your neck.

40) One wallet and one pair of shoes, one color, all seasons.

41) You can do your nails with a pocket-knife.

42) You have freedom of choice concerning growing a mustache.

43) Christmas shopping can be accomplished for 25 relatives, December 24th in 45 minutes.

44) The world is your urinal.

♦   ♦   ♦

P O O F! ♦ ♦ ♦ ♦ ♦ ♦ ♦ ♦

One day, three men were hiking and unexpectedly came upon a large raging violent river. They needed to get to the other side, but had no idea of how to do so. The first man prayed to God, saying, "Please God, give me the strength to cross this river." **Poof!** God gave him big arms and strong legs, and he was able to swim across the river in about two hours, after almost drowning a couple of times.

Seeing this, the second man prayed to God, saying "Please God, give me the strength .. and the tools to cross this river." **Poof!** God gave him a rowboat and he was able to row across the river in about an hour, after almost capsizing the boat a couple of times.

The third man had seen how this worked out for the other two, so he also prayed to God saying, "Please God, give me the strength and the tools ... and the intelligence ... to cross this river." And **Poof!** God turned him into a woman. She looked at the map, hiked upstream a couple of hundred yards, then walked across the bridge!

♦   ♦   ♦   ♦   ♦   ♦   ♦   ♦

Actual Signs Found in Bathrooms Along the Way . . . . .

Friends don't let friends take home ugly men.
(Women's restroom, Starboard, Dewey Beach, DE)

Remember, it's not, "How high are you?", it's "Hi, how are you?"
(Rest stop off Route 81, WV)

No matter how good she looks, some other guy is stick and
  tired of putting up with her shit.
  (Men's Room, Linda's Bar and Grill, Chapel Hill, NC)

A Woman's rule of Thumb: If it has tires or testicles, you're
  going to have trouble with it.
  (Women's restroom, Dick's Last Resort, Dallas, TX)

Express Lane: Five beers or less.
  (Sign over one of the urinals, Ed Debevic's, Beverly Hills, CA)

You're too good for him.
  (Sign over mirror, women's room, Ed Debevic's, Beverly Hills,
  CA)

No wonder you always go home alone.
  (Sign over mirror in Men's room, Ed Debevic's Beverly Hills,
  CA)

The best way to a man's heart is to saw his breast plate open.
  (Women's restroom, Murphy's, Champaign, IL)

Beauty is only a light switch away.
  (Perkins Library, Duke University, Durham, NC)

If life is a waste of time, and time is a waste of life, then let's all
  get wasted together and have the time of our lives.
  (Armand's Pizza, Washington, D.C.)

Don't trust anything that bleeds for 5 days and doesn't die.
  (Men's restroom, Murphy's, Champaign, IL)

What are you looking up on the wall for? The joke is in your
  hands.
  (Men's restroom, Lynagh's, Lexington, KY)

"When I Created the Heavens and the Earth, I Spoke Them Into Being."

When I created man, I formed him and breathed life into his nostrils.

But you, woman, I fashioned after I breathed the breath of life into man, because your nostrils are too delicate. I allowed a deep sleep to come over him so I could patiently and perfectly fashion you. Man was put to sleep so that he could not interfere with the creativity.

From one bone, I fashioned you. I chose the bone that protects man's life. I chose the rib, which protects his heart and lungs and supports him, as you are meant to do. Around this one bone, I shaped you, I modeled you. I created you perfectly and beautifully. Your characteristics are as the rib, strong yet delicate and fragile. You provide protection for the most delicate organ in man, his heart. His heart is the center of his being; his lungs hold the breath of life. The ribcage will allow itself to be broken before it will allow damage to the heart.

Support man as the rib cage supports the body. You were not taken from his feet, to be under him, nor were you taken from his head, to be above him. You were taken from his side, to stand beside him and be held close to his side.

You are my perfect Angel . . . . . you are my beautiful little girl. You have grown to be a splendid woman of excellence, and my eyes fill when I see the virtues in your heart. Your eyes . . . . . don't change them. Your lips – how lovely when they part in prayer. Your nose, so perfect in form. Your hands so gentle to touch. I've caressed your face in your deepest sleep. I've held your heart close to mine. Of all that lives and breathes, you are most like me.

Her Diary:

He was in an odd mood when I got to the bar; I thought it might have been because I was a bit late but he didn't say anything much about it. The conversation was quite slow going, so I thought we should go off somewhere more intimate so we could talk more privately. So we went to his restaurant and he's STILL acting a bit funny and I'm trying to cheer him up and start to wonder whether it's me or something else. I ask him, and he says no. but you know I'm not really sure. So anyway, in the cab back to his house, I say that I love him and he just puts his arm around me. I don't know what the hell this means because you know he doesn't say it back or anything. We finally get back to this place and I'm wondering if he's going to dump me! So I try to ask him about it but he just switches on the TV. Reluctantly, I say I'm going to go to sleep. Then, after about 10 minutes, he joins me and we have sex, But, he still seemed really distracted, so afterwards I just wanted to leave. I dun'no, I just don't know what he thinks anymore. I mean, do you think he's met someone else???

His Diary:

Shitty day at work.. Tired. Got laid though.

SUBJECT: Salary Raise

I, the penis, hereby request a raise in salary for the following reasons:

- ❖   I do physical labor
- ❖   I work at great depths
- ❖   I work head first
- ❖   I do not get weekends off or public holidays
- ❖   I work in a damp environment

❖ I don't get paid overtime or shift penalties

❖ I work in a dark workplace that has poor ventilation

❖ I work in high temperatures

❖ My work exposes me to contagious diseases

<u>Response from the Administration:</u>

After assessing your request and considering the arguments you have raised, the Administration rejects your request for the following reasons:

❖ You do not work 8 hours straight

❖ You fall asleep on the job after brief work periods

❖ You do not always follow the orders of the management team

❖ You do not stay in your allocated position, and often visit other areas

❖ You take a lot of non-rostered breaks

❖ You do not take initiative – you need to be pressured and stimulated in order to start working

❖ You leave the workplace rather messy at the end of your sift

❖ You don't always observe Health & Safety measures, such as wearing the correct protective outfits

❖ You don't wait till pension age before retiring

❖ You don't like working double shifts

❖ You sometimes leave your allocated position before you have completed the day's work

❖   And if that were not all, you have been seen constantly entering and leaving the work place carrying 2 suspicious looking bags.

Subject: What Kind of Penis Do You or Your Man Have?

The Excedrin Penis: It's tthhhhiiiiiiiiisssss big.

The Snickers Penis: It satisfies you.

The Life Call Penis: It's fallen and it can't get up.

The American Express Penis: Don't leave hoe without it.

The Tootsie Roll Pop Penis: How many licks DOES it take . . .?

The M&M Penis: Melts in your mouth, not in your hand.

The Lucky Charms Penis: It's magically delicious.

The Energizer Penis: It keeps going and going.

The Right Guard Penis: Anything less is uncivilized.

The Campbell's Soup Penis: mmm mmm good.

The Kix Penis: Kid tested, mother approved.

The McDonald's Penis: Over 8 billion served.

The Tombstone Penis: What would you like on your penis?

The Allstate Penis: You're in good hands.

The Barq's Penis: The one with bite.

The Beef Penis: It's what's for dinner.

The Bud Lite Penis: Great taste, less filling.

The Transformers Penis: It's more than meets the eye.

The Twizzler Penis: It makes mouths happy.

The Starburst Penis: The juice is loose.

The Timex Penis: Takes a lickin' and keeps on ....

The Burger King Penis: It takes two hands to handle a whopper.

The Wendy's Penis: Where's the beef?

The Lays Penis: Betcha can't eat just one.

The Bounty Penis: The quicker picker-upper.

The Street Fighter II Penis: Matt, stop, you're too good at this.

The Domino's Pizza Penis: Delivers in 30 minutes or less.

The Rice Krispies Penis: What does your penis say to you?

The Extra Penis: Last an extra, extra, extra long time.

The Charmin Penis: Don't squeeze the penis!

The Beatles Penis: Now a quarter smaller than it used to be.

The Windows '95 Penis: If you ask it to do too much, it'll crash.

The Virginia Slims Penis: You've come a long way, baby.

The Secret Penis: Strong enough for a man, ph balanced for a woman.

The Micro Machines Penis: A whole world, in the palm of your hand.

The Sanka Penis: Good to the last drop.

The Payday Penis: It's almost totally nuts!

The Yellow Pages Penis: Let your fingers do the walkin'.

The Sustecal Penis: More protein, less fat!

The Milk Penis: It does a body good!

The Cinnamon Toast Crunch Penis: It's the adult thing to do.

The AOL Penis: It's so easy to use, no wonder it's #1?

The Pontiac Penis: Built for kicks, Built for Keeps!

The Psychic Penis: It knows you are coming before you do.

The Chevrolet Penis: Like a Rock!

Expressions for Women on High Stress Days ....

1) You! – off my planet.

2) Not the brightest crayon in the box now, are we?

3) Well, this day was a total waste of makeup.

4) Errors have been made. Others will be blamed.

5) And your crybaby whiny-assed opinion would be ... ?

6) I'm not crazy, I've just been in a very bad mood for 30 years.

7) Allow me to introduce my selves.

8) Sarcasm is just one more service we offer.

9) Whatever kind of look you were going for, you missed.

10) I'm just working here till a good fast-food job opens up.

11) I'm trying to imagine you with a personality.

12) Stress is when you wake up screaming and you realize you weren't asleep.

13) I can't remember if I'm the good twin or the evil one.

14) How many times do I have to flush before you go away?

15) I just want revenge. Is that so wrong?

16) You say I'm a bitch like it's a bad thing.

17) Can I trade this job for what's behind door #2?

18) Nice perfume. Must you marinate in it?

19) Chaos, panic + disorder – my work here is done.

20) Earth is full. Go home.

21) Is it time for your medication or mine?

22) How do I set a laser printer to stun?

23)   I'm not tense, just terribly, terribly alert.

Politically Correct Terms for Women

SHE DOES NOT: GET PMS.
SHE BECOMES: HORMONALLY HOMICICAL.

SHE DOES NOT HAVE: A KILLER BODY
SHE IS: TERMINALLY ATTRACTIVE.

SHE IS: A BAD COOK.
SHE IS: MICROWAVE COMPATIBLE.

SHE IS: A BAD DRIVER.
SHE IS: AUTOMOTIVELY CHALLENGED.

SHE IS NOT: A PERFECT 10.
SHE IS: NUMERICALLY SUPERIOR.

SHE IS NOT: EASY.
SHE IS: HORIZONTALLY ACCESSIBLE.

SHE DOES NOT: HATE SPORTS ON TV.
SHE IS: ATHLETICALLY BIASED.

SHE DOES NOT: HAVE SEXY LIPS
SHE IS: COLLAGEN DEPENDENT.

SHE DOES NOT: GET DRUNK.
SHE IS: ACCIDENTALLY OVER SERVED.

YOU DO NOT ASK HER: TO DANCE.
YOU REQUEST: A PRECOITAL RHYTHMIC
EXPERIENCE.

SHE IS NOT: A GOSSIP.
SHE IS A: VERBAL TERMINATOR.

SHE DOES NOT: WORK OUT TOO MUCH.
SHE IS AN: ABDOMINAL OVER-ACHIEVER.

SHE DOES NOT HAVE A: GREAT BUTT.
SHE IS: GLUTEUS TO THE MAXIMUS

SHE IS NOT: HOOKED ON SOAP OPERAS.
SHE IS: MELODRAMATICALLY FIXATED.

SHE IS NOT: COLD OR FRIGID.
SHE IS: THERMALLY INCOMPATIBLE.

SHE DOES NOT: WEAR TOO MUCH MAKEUP.
SHE IS: COSMETICALY OVER-SATURATED.

SHE DOES NOT HAVE: GREAT CLEAVAGE (A
GREAT RACK)
HER BREASTS ARE: CENTRALLY LOCATED.

SHE WILL NEVER: GAIN WEIGHT.
SHE WILL BECOME: A METABOLIC UNDER-
ACHIEVER..

SHE IS NOT: A SCREAMER OR MOANER.
SHE IS : VOCALLY APPRECIATIVE.

SHE DOES NOT: SHAVE HER LEGS.
SHE EXPERIENCES: TEMPORARY STUBBLE
REDUCTION.

SHE DOES NOT HAVE: A HARD BODY.
SHE IS: ANATOMICALLY INFLEXIBLE.

SHE DOES NOT: SUN BATHE.
SHE EXPERIENCES: SOLAR ENHANCEMENT.

HER BREASTS WILL NEVER: SAG.
THEY WILL: LOSE THEIR VERTICAL HOLD.

SHE DOES NOT: SHOP TOO MUCH.
SHE IS: OVERLY SUCEPTIBLE TO MARKETING
PLOYS.

SHE DOES NOT: CUT YOU OFF.
SHE BECOMES: HORIZONTALLY INACCESSIBLE.

SHE DOES NOT HAVE: BIG HAIR.
SHE IS: OVERLY AEROSOLED.

SHE DOES NOT: SNORE.
SHE IS: NASALLY REPETITIVE.

SHE DOES NOT: GET DRUNK.
SHE BECOMES: VERBALLY DYSLEXIC.

SHE DOES NOT HAVE: BIG HOOTERS.
HER: CUPS RUNNETH OVER.

The Top 10 Reasons Why E-Mail is Like a Male Reproductive Organ:

10. Those who have it would be devastated if it were ever cut off.

9. Those who have it think that those who don't are somehow inferior.

8. Those who don't have it may agree that it's neat, but think it's not worth the fuss that those who have it make about it.

7. Many of those who don't have it would like to try it (e-mail envy).

6. It's more fun when it's up but this makes it hard to get any real work done.

5. In the distant past, its only purpose was to transmit information vital to the survival of the species. Some people still think that's the only thing it should be used for, but most folks today use it for fun most of the time.

4. If you don't apply the appropriate measures, it can spread viruses.

3. If you use it too much, you'll find it becomes more and more difficult to think coherently.

2. We attach an importance to it that is far greater than its actual size and influence warrant.

1. If you're not careful what you do with it, it can get you into a lot of trouble.

So Which Condom Would You Use ...?

⇨   Nike Condoms: Just do it.

⇨   Toyota Condoms: Oh what a feeling.

⇨   Diet Pepsi condoms: You got the right one, baby.

⇨   Pringles Condoms: Once you pop, you can't stop.

⇨   Mentos Condoms: The freshmaker.

⇨   Flintstones Vitamins Condom: Ten million strong and growing.

⇨   Secret condoms: Strong enough for a man, but pH balanced for a woman.

⇨   Macintosh Condoms: It does more, it costs less, it's that simple.

⇨ Ford condoms: The best never rest.

⇨ Chevy Condoms: Like a rock.

⇨ Dial Condoms: Aren't you glad you use it? Don't you wish everybody did?

⇨ New York Lotto Condoms: 'Cause hey – you never know.

⇨ California Lotto condoms: Who's next?

⇨ Avis Condoms: Trying harder than ever.

⇨ KFC Condoms: Finger-Licking Good.

⇨ Coca Cola Condoms: Always the Real Thing.

⇨ Lays Condoms: Betcha can't have just one.

⇨ Campbell's Soup Condoms: Mmm, mmm, good.

⇨ General Electric Condoms: We bring good things to life!

⇨ AT&T Condoms: Reach out and touch someone.

⇨ Bounty Condoms: The quicker picker upper.

⇨ Microsoft Condoms: Where do you want to go today?

⇨ Energizer Condoms: It keeps going and going, and going . . . .

⇨ M&M Condoms: It melts in your mouth, not in your hands!

⇨ Taco Bell Condoms: Get some; make a run for the border.

⇨ MCI Condoms: For friends and family.

⇨ Doublemint Condoms: Double your pleasure, double your fun!

⇨ The Sears Latex Condoms: One coat is good for the entire winter.

⇨ Delta Airlines Travel Pack Condoms: Delta is ready when you are.

⇨ United Airlines travel pack Condoms: Fly united.

⇨ The Star Trek Condoms: To boldly go where no man has gone before.

Here's One for the Ladies:

- Men are like ... Placemats.
- They only show up when there's food on the table.

- Men are like ... Mascara.
- They usually run at the first sign of emotion.

- Men are like ... bike helmets.
- Handy in an emergency, but otherwise they just look silly.

- Men are like ... Government bonds.
- They take so long to mature.

- Men are needed for one thing . . . . .
- But the car doesn't have to be fixed all the time.

- Men are like ... Lava lamps.
- Fun to look at, but not all that bright.

- Men are like ... Bank accounts
- Without a lot of money, they don't generate much interest.

◆ Men are like . . . High heels.

◆ They're easy to walk on once you get the hang of it.

20 Ways to Say "Your Fly is Open" !

1) The cucumber has left the salad.

2) I can see the gun of Navarone.

3) Someone tore down the wall, and your Pink Floyd is hanging out.

4) You've got Windows in your laptop.

5) Sailor Ned's trying to take a little shore leave.

6) Your soldier ain't so unknown now.

7) Quasimodo needs to go back in the tower and tend to his bell.

8) Paging Mr. Johnson. . . Paging Mr. Johnson . . .

9) You need to bring your tray table to the upright and locked position.

10) Your pod bay door is open, Hal.

11) Elvis Junior has LEFT the building!

12) Mini Me is making a break for the escape pod.

13) Ensign Hanes is reporting a hull breach on the lower deck, Sir!

14) The Buick is not all the way in the garage.

15) Dr. Kimble has escaped!

16) You've got your fly set for "Monica" instead of "Hillary."

17) Our next guest is someone who needs no introduction . . .

18) You've got a security breach at Los Pant alones.

19) I'm talking about Shaft, can you dig it?

20) I thought you were crazy; now I see your nuts!

⏮   ⏮   ⏮   ⏮ ⏭   ⏭   ⏭   ⏭

The Top Ten Reasons Why Trick-Or-Treating Is Better Than Sex !?!?

10. Guaranteed to get at least a little something in the sack.

9. If you get tired, wait 10 minutes and go at it again.

8. The uglier you look, the easier it is to get some.

7. You don't have to compliment the person who gave you candy.

6. Person giving you candy doesn't fantasize you're someone else.

5. If you get a stomach ache, it won't last 9 months.

4. If you wear your Batman mask, no one thinks you're kinky.

3. Doesn't matter if kids hear you moaning and groaning.

2. Less guilt the next morning . . .

#1. If you don't get what you want, you can always go next door!

WOMEN'S ENGLISH:

Yes	=	No
No	=	Yes
Maybe	=	No

I'm sorry	=	You'll be sorry
We need	=	I want
It's your decision	=	The correct decision should be obvious by now
Do what you want	=	You'll pay for this later
We need to talk	=	I need to complain
Sure... go ahead	=	I don't want you to
I'm not upset	=	Of course I'm upset, you moron!
You're ... so manly	=	You need a shave and you sweat a lot.
You're certainly attentive tonight	=	Is sex all you ever thing about?
Be romantic, turn out the lights	=	I have flabby thighs
This kitchen is so inconvenient	=	I want a new house
I want new curtains	=	And carpeting, and furniture, and wallpaper....
Hang the picture there	=	NO, I mean hang it there!
I heard a noise	=	I noticed you were almost asleep
Do you love me?	=	I'm going to ask for something expensive
How much do you love me?	=	I did something today you're really not going to like
I'll be ready in a minute	=	Kick off your shoes and find a good game on TV
Is my butt fat?	=	Tell me I'm beautiful
You have to learn to communicate	=	Just agree with me
Are you listening to me!?	=	[Too late, you're dead]

Was that the baby?	=	Why don't you get out of bed & walk him to sleep
I'm not yelling!	=	Yes, I am yelling because I think this is important
The same old thing	=	Nothing
Nothing	=	Everything
Everything	=	My PMS is acting up
Nothing, really	=	It's just that you're such an asshole

MEN'S ENGLISH:

I'm hungry	=	I'm hungry
I'm sleepy	=	I'm sleepy
I'm tired	=	I'm tired
Do you want to go to a movie?	=	I'd eventually like to have sex with you
Can I take you out to dinner?	=	I'd eventually like to have sex with you
Can I call you sometime?	=	I'd eventually like to have sex with you
May I have this dance?	=	I'd eventually like to have sex with you
Can I get your coat?	=	I'd eventually like to have sex with you
Let me get your door.	=	I'd eventually like to have sex with you
Nice dress!"	=	Nice cleavage!

You look tense, let me give you a massage = I want to fondle you

What's wrong? = I guess sex tonight is out of the question

What's wrong? = What meaningless self-inflicted psychological trauma are you going through now?

What's wrong? = I don't see why you're making such a big deal about this

Good morning = That was great sex .. Let's have more

See you later = That was great sex .. Let's have more

I'm bored = Do you want to have sex?

I love you = Let's have sex now

I love you, too = Okay, I said it ... we'd better have sex now!

Yes, I like the way you cut your hair = I liked it better before you cut it

Yes, I like the way you cut your hair = $50 and it doesn't look that much different

Let's talk = I am trying to impress you by showing that I am a deep person and maybe then you'd like to have sex with me

Will you marry me? = I want to make it illegal for you to have sex with other guys

Will you marry me? = I might as well get tax benefits for going thru these talks

(While shopping) I like that one better = Pick any freakin' dress and let's go home!

I don't think that blouse and that skirt go well together. = I'm gay

WOMEN'S AGES:

≈ Between the ages of 13 and 18, she is like Africa ... virgin and unexplored.

≈ Between the ages of 19 and 35, she is like Asia ... hot and exotic.

≈ Between the ages of 36 and 45, she is like America ... fully explored breathtakingly beautiful, and free with her resources.

≈ Between the ages of 46 and 58, she is like Europe ... exhausted, but still has many points of interest.

≈ After 58, she is like Australia . . everybody knows it's down there, but who gives a damn.

MEN'S AGES:

↔ Between the ages of 18 and 32 ... Tri – weekly.

↔ Between the ages of 32 and 50 ... Tri – weekly.

↔ Over 50 ... Try, weakly.

If Men Were in Charge of Weddings . . . . .

There would be a "Rehearsal Dinner Kegger" until the cops showed up. Bridesmaids would wear matching blue jean cut-offs and halter tops. They would have NO tan lines and more skin showing than not... tuxes would have team logos on the back and the Nike shoes would have matching team colors .. The bride's dress would show cleavage, her navel, and be form-fitted to her ass. No one would bother with that "Veil routine". But they would insist that the garter be as high up on her leg as it could go. The bridal bouquet would be recycled from a previous funeral/wedding (what's the difference) or something.

Big, slobbery dogs would be eligible for the role of "Best Man".

June weddings would be scheduled around basketball play-offs. Vows would mention cooking and sex specifically, but omit that "forsaking all others" part.

Outdoor weddings would be held during sporting events at half-time or between innings. Ceremonies would be short and honey-moons would be long. Ceremonies and honeymoons would be in-expensive compared to the cost of the bachelor party. The cost of the strippers and liquor really do add up .

Instead of a sit-down dinner or a buffet, there would be a hog roast or buckets of chicken, pizza and plenty of bar-b-que. There would be "Tailgate Receptions." Idiots who tried to dance with the bride (unless they were really old) would get punched in the head. The couple would leave the ceremony in a souped up '73 Charger or some other Mopar with racing tires and flame designs on the side of the car. Better yet, a Harley!

Men wouldn't ask, "Well, what do you think, Dear? The burgundy or the wine colored napkins?" They'd just grab extras from their local pub or tavern. Favors would be matchbooks and cigars. Better yet, free drink passes at the local lounge. The invitations would read as follows ..."Tom (Dick or Harry) is getting the old ball and chain .. . He's getting married. He either
knocked her up, (B) Couldn't get a different roommate or, (C) Caved in to her ultimatum... Please meet the woman who will cook and clean for him for the rest of his life at Soldier Field Stadium on the 50-yard line at half-time during Sunday's game. Please join us at the Moonlight Lounge after the game for beer, nachos, and pizza. Oh, yeah .. B.Y.O.B."

ONE-HUNDRED Reasons Why It's Great to be a Woman !

Free dinners

Free lunches

Free brunches

Free movies (you get the point)

You can hug your friend without wondering if she thinks you're gay

You can cry without pretending there's something in your contact

You know the truth about whether size matters

Speeding Ticket? What's that?

You can hug your friend without wondering if YOU're gay

You actually get extra points for sitting on your butt watching sports

You don't have to try to laugh louder, deeper and harder than your buddy

If you never have a son, it's okay

If you do have a son, and he's a lousy athlete, it's still okay

If YOU're a lousy athlete, you don't have to question your worth as a human being

A new lipstick gives you a whole new lease on life

In high school, you never had to walk down the hall with your binder strategically positioned

If you have sex with someone and don't call them the next day, it doesn't mean you're the devil

You don't have to count how many people you've slept with

Condoms make no significant difference in your enjoyment of sex

I Need a Copy of That

If you have to be home in time for 90210, you can say so, out loud

If you're not making enough money, you can blame the glass ceiling

You can sleep your way to the top

You can sue for sexual harassment

You can sue the President for sexual harassment

If you're not very attractive, you can fool 'em with makeup

If you use self-tanner, it doesn't necessarily mean you're a big loser

Same with tanning beds

Nothing crucial can be cut off with one clean sweep

You could possibly live your whole life without ever taking a group shower

You can get free stuff just by smiling sweetly

If you're pregnant, YOU get to decide what to do about it

Brad Pitt

You don't have to fart to amuse yourself

If you cheat on your spouse, people assume it's because you're being emotionally neglected

You never have to wonder if your orgasm was real

You'll never have to decide where to hide your nose-hair clipper

When you take off your shoes, nobody passes out

If the person you're dating is much better at something than you are, you don't have to break up with them

If you think the person you're dating really likes you, you don't have to break up with them

Excitement is only as far away as the nearest drug/beauty-aid store

If you don't shave, no one will know

You can congratulate your teammate without ever touching her ass

If you have a zit, you can conceal it

You don't have to reach down every so often to make sure your privates are still there

If you want to have sex, you always can

If you're dumb, some people will find it cute

You don't have to memorize Caddyshack or Fletch to fit in

If you love someone, it's easy for you to tell them

Your hair is yours to keep

If you ARE bald, people will think you did it on purpose, and you're really chic

Once a month, you have an excuse to be a total bitch

You don't need a special occasion to hug your dad

You never have to wonder if you'll offend someone by opening the door for them

When necessary, you can live without sex

You can always get a ride hitchhiking

You don't have to pretend to like cigars

You don't have to pretend you liked cigars before they were cool

You'll never have to blow 2 months salary on anything

You can talk to people of the opposite sex without having to picture them naked

If you marry someone 20 years younger, you know you look like an idiot

You don't think that wearing a warm coat in the dead of winter makes you look like a wuss

I Need a Copy of That

You're rarely compelled to scream at the TV

If you wear cologne, you don't have to pretend it's aftershave

You'll probably never see someone you know while peeing in an alley

You never have to punch a hole through anything with your fist

You don't have a scar right under your chin

You and your friends don't have to get totally wasted in order to share your feelings

If you talk to your mom every day, it's normal

If you pick up the check once in a while, that's plenty

Sitting and watching people is all the entertainment you need

You can quickly end any fight simply by crying

You can decide not to work once you've had kids

When you get a million catalogues in the mail, it's a good thing

Sometimes, chocolate truly can solve all your problems

If you're under 6 feet tall, you don't have to lie about it

You have never had a goatee

Gay waiters don't make you uncomfortable

You'll never regret piercing your ears

You can fully assess someone just by looking at their shoes

You'll never discover you've been fooled by a Wonderbra

When you wear sweatpants, it isn't obscene

You know better than to ever use Grecian Formula

It doesn't take you an hour to go to the bathroom

You don't have hair on your back

Your doctor never has to put on a rubber glove

When you get dumped, you can admit you're depressed

If anything on your body isn't as big as it should be, you can get implants

You can tell which glass was yours by the lipstick mark

If you have big ears, no one has to know

If someone takes your seat in a bar, you don't have to hit them

It's okay if you can't drive stick shift

Ally McBeal

You get to hate Kathie Lee in the way only another woman truly can

You can be attracted to someone just because they're really funny

You can borrow your spouse's clothes and it doesn't mean you belong on Jerry Springer Show

You've known the joy of making a collage for your BFF

You bond easily

When you become President, you'll be the first woman ever

100 Things
NOT TO SAY During Sex

1. But everybody looks funny naked!

2. You woke me up for that!

3. Did I mention the video camera?

4. Do you smell something burning?

5. (In a janitor's closet) And they say romance is dead ...

6. Try breathing through your nose.

7. A little rug burn never hurt anyone!

8. Is that a Medic Alert pendant?

9. Sweetheart, did you lock the back door?

10. But whipped cream makes me break out.

11. Person 1: This is your first time...right?

   Person 2: Yeah .. today.

12. (In the No-Tell Motel) Hurry up! This room rents by the hour!

13. Can you please pass me the remote control?

14. Do you accept Visa?

15. ZZZZZZZZZZZZZZZZZZZZZZZZZZZZZZZZZZ

16. On second thought, let's turn off the lights.

17. And to think – I was really trying to pick up your friend!

18. So much for mouth-to-mouth.

19. (Using body paint) Try not to leave any stains, okay?

20. Hope you're as good looking when I'm sober ...

21. (Holding a banana) It's just a little trick I learned at the zoo!

22. Do you get any premium movie channels?

23. Try not to smear my make-up, will ya!

24. (Preparing to use peanut butter sexually) But I just steam-cleaned this couch!

25. Got any penicillin?

26. But I just brushed my teeth . . .

27. Smile, you're on Candid Camera!

28. I though you had the keys to the handcuffs!

29. I want a baby!

30. So much for the fulfillment of sexual fantasies!

31. (In a mÈnage a trios) Why am I doing all the work?

32. Maybe we should call Dr. Ruth . . .

33. Did you know the ceiling needs painting?

34. I think you have it on backwards.

35. When is this supposed to feel good?

36. Put that blender back in the kitchen where it belongs!

37. You're good enough to do this for a living!

38. Is that blood on the headboard?

39. Did I remember to take my pill?

40. Are you sure I don't know you from somewhere?

41. I wish we got the Playboy channel ...

42. That leak better be from the waterbed!

43. I told you it wouldn't work without batteries!

44. But my cat always sleeps on that pillow ..

45. Did I tell you my Aunt Martha died in this bed?

46. If you quit smoking you might have more endurance ...

47. No, really ... I do this part better myself!

48. It's nice being in bed with a woman I don't have to inflate!

49. This would be more fun with a few more people...

50. You're almost as good as my ex!

51. Do you know the definition of statutory rape?

52. Is that you I smell or is it your mattress stuffed with something rotten?

53. You look younger than you feel.

54. Perhaps you're just out of practice.

55. You sweat more than a galloping stallion!

56. They're not cracker crumbs, it's just a rash.

57. Now I know why he/she dumped you ...

58. Does your husband own a sawed-off shot gun?

59. You give me reason to conclude that foreplay is over-rated.

60. What tampon?

61. Have you ever considered liposuction?

62. And to think, I didn't even have to buy you dinner!

63. What are you planning to make for breakfast?

64. I have a confession ...

65. I was so horny tonight I would have taken a duck home!

66. Are those real or am I just behind the times?

67. Were you by any chance repressed as a child?

68. Is that a hanging sculpture?

69. You'll still vote for me, won't you?

70. Did I mention my transsexual operation?

71. I really hate women who actually think sex means something!

72. Did you come yet, dear?

73. I'll tell you who I'm fantasizing about if you tell me who you're fantasizing about

74. A good plastic surgeon can take care of that in no time?

75. Does this count as a date?

76. Oprah Winfrey had a show about men like you!

77. Hic! I need another beer for this please.

78. I think biting is romantic, don't you?

79. Q: You can cook, too right?   A: Whaddaya think I'm doing?

80. When would you like to meet my parents?

81. Man: Maybe it would help if I thought about someone I really like.   Woman: Yourself?!

82. Have you seen "Fatal Attraction"?

83. Sorry about the name tags, I'm not very good with names

84. Don't mind me .. I always file my nails in bed.

85. (In a phone booth) Do you mind if I make a few phone calls?

86. I hope I didn't forget to turn the gas oven off. Do you have a light?

87. Don't worry, my dog's really friendly for a Doberman.

88. Sorry but I don't do toes!

89. You could at least ACT like you're enjoying it.

90. Petroleum jelly or no petroleum jelly, I said NO!

91. Keep it down, my mother is a light sleeper ...

92. I'll bet you didn't know I work for "The Enquirer".

93. So that's why they call you MR. Flash!!

94. My old girlfriend used to do it a LOT longer!

95. Is this a sin too?

96. I've slept with more women than Wilt Chamberlain!

97. Long kisses clog my sinuses ...

98. Please understand that I'm only doing this for a raise ...

99. How long do you plan to be "almost there"?

100. You mean you're NOT my blind date?

"TEN SIMPLE RULES FOR DATING MY DAUGHTER"

Some thoughtful information for those who are daughters, were daughters, have daughters, intend to have daughters, or intend to date a daughter!

Rule One: If you pull into my driveway and honk you'd better be delivering a package, because you're sure not picking anything up.

Rule Two: You do not touch my daughter in front of me. You may glance at her, so long as you do not peer at anything below her neck. If you cannot keep your eyes or hands off of my daughter's body, I will remove them.

Rule Three: I am aware that its is considered fashionable for boys of your age to wear their trousers so loosely that they appear to be falling off their hips. Please don't take this as an insult, but you and all of your friends are complete idiots. Still, I want to be fair and open minded about this issue, so I propose this compromise: You may come to the door with your underwear showing and your pants ten sizes too big, and I will not object. However, In order to ensure that your clothes do not, in fact, come off during the course of your date with my daughter, I will take my electric nail gun and fasten your trousers securely in place to your waist.

Rule Four: I'm sure you've been told that in today's world, sex without utilizing a "barrier method" of some kind can kill you. Let me elaborate: when it comes to sex, I am the barrier, and I will kill you.

Rule Five: In order for us to get to know each other, we should talk about sports, politics, and other issues of the day. Please do not do this. The only information I require from you is an indication of when you expect to have my daughter safely back at my house, and the only word I need from you on this subject is "early".

Rule Six: I have no doubt you are a popular fellow, with many opportunities to date other girls. This is fine with me as long as it is okay with my daughter. Otherwise, once you have gone out with my little girl, you will continue to date no one but her until she is finished with you. If you make her cry, I will make you cry.

Rule Seven: As you stand in my front hallway, waiting for my daughter to appear, and more than an hour goes by, do not sigh and fidget.

If you want to be on time for the movie, you should not be dating. My daughter is putting on her makeup, a process that can take longer than painting the Golden Gate Bridge. Instead of just standing there, why don't you do something useful, like change the oil in my car?

Rule Eight: The following places are not appropriate for a date with my daughter: Places where there are beds, sofas, or anything softer than a wooden stool. Places where there are no parents, policemen, or nuns within eyesight. Places where there is darkness. Places where there is dancing, holding hands, or happiness. Places where the ambient temperature is warm enough to induce my daughter to wear shorts, tank tops, midriff T-shirts, or anything other than overalls, a sweater, and a goose down parka zipped up to her throat. Movies with a strong romantic or sexual theme are to be avoided; movies which feature chainsaws are okay. Hockey games are okay. Old folks home are better.

Rule Nine: Do not lie to me. I may appear to be a pot-bellied, balding, middle-aged, dim-witted has-been, but on issues relating to my daughter, I am the all-knowing, merciless god of your universe. If I ask you where you are going and with whom, you have one chance to tell me the truth, the whole truth, and nothing but the truth. I have a shotgun, a shovel, and five acres behind the house. Do not trifle with me.

Rule Ten: Be afraid. Be very afraid. It takes very little for me to mistake the sound of your car in the driveway for a chopper coming in over a rice paddy outside of Hanoi. When my Agent Orange starts acting up, the voices in my head frequently tell me to clean the guns as I wait for you to bring my daughter home. As soon as you pull into the driveway you should exit your car with both hands in plain sight. Speak the perimeter password, announce in a clear voice that you have brought my daughter home safely and early, then return to your car. There is no need for you to come inside. The camouflaged face at the window is mine.

TOP TWENTY REASONS WHY CHOCOLATE IS BETTER THAN SEX:

First: You can GET chocolate.

Second: "If you love me you'll swallow that" has real meaning with chocolate.

Third: Chocolate satisfies even when it has gone soft.

Fourth: You can safely have chocolate while you are driving.

Fifth: You can make chocolate last as long as you want it to.

Sixth: You can have chocolate, even in front of your mother.

Seventh: If you bite the nuts too hard, the chocolate won't mind.

Eighth: Two people of the same sex can have chocolate without being called nasty names.

Ninth: The word "commitment" doesn't scare off chocolate.

Tenth: You can have chocolate on top of your workbench/desk during working hours without upsetting your work mates.

Eleventh: You can ask a stranger for chocolate without getting your face slapped.

Twelfth: You don't get hairs in your mouth with chocolate.

Thirteenth: With chocolate, there's no need to fake it.

Fourteenth: Chocolate doesn't make you pregnant.

Fifteenth: You can have chocolate at any time of the month.

Sixteenth: Good chocolate is easy to find.

Seventeenth: You can have as many kinds of chocolate as you can handle.

Eighteenth: You are never too young or too old for chocolate.

Nineteenth: When you have chocolate, it does not keep your neighbors awake.

Twentieth: With chocolate size doesn't matter; it's always good.

A PERFECT DAY FOR A MAN:

6:00	Alarm
6:15	Blowjob
6:30	Massive dump while reading the sports section
7:00	Breakfast. Filet Mignon, eggs, toast & coffee
7:30	Limo arrives
7:45	Bloody Mary en route to airport
8:15	Private jet to Augusta, Georgia
9:30	Limo to Augusta National Golf club
9:45	Play front nine at Augusta; finish 2 under par
11:45	Lunch; 2-dozen oysters on the half shell, 3 Heinekens
12:15	Blowjob
12:30	Play back nine at Augusta; finish 4 under par
2:15	Limo back to airport; drink 2 Bombay martinis
2:30	Private jet to Nassau, Bahamas; nap
3:15	Late afternoon fishing excursion with topless female crew
4:30	Catch world record light tackle marlin – 1249 lbs.
5:00	Jet back home. En route, get massage from naked supermodel
6:30	Blowjob
7:00	Watch CNN Newsflash; Clinton resigns

7:30	Dinner: Lobster appetizers, 1963 Dom Perignon, 20 oz. New York strip
9:00	Relax after dinner with 1789 Augler cognac and Cohiba Cuban cigar
10:00	Have sex with two 18-year-old nymphomaniacs
11:00	Massage and Jacuzzi
11:45	Go to bed
11:50	Let loose a 12 second, 4 octave fart; watch the dog leave the room
11:55	Laugh yourself to sleep.

A PERFECT DAY FOR A WOMAN:

8:15	Wake up to hugs and kisses
8:30	Weigh 5 lbs lighter than yesterday
8:45	Breakfast in bed, fresh squeezed orange juice and croissants
9:15	Soothing hot bath with fragrant lilac bath oil
10:00	Light workout at club with handsome, funny personal trainer
10:30	Facial, manicure, shampoo, and comb out
12:00	Lunch with best friend at an outdoor cafÈ
12:45	Notice ex-boyfriend's wife, she has gained 30 lbs ..
1:00	Shopping with friends
3:00	Nap
4:00	A dozen roses delivered by florist; card is from a secret admirer
4:15	Light workout at club followed by a gentle massage
5:30	Pick outfit for dinner. Primp before mirror
7:30	Candlelight dinner for two followed by dancing
10:00	Hot shower, alone
10:30	Make love

| 11:00 | Pillow talk, light touching and cuddling |
| 11:15 | Fall asleep in his big, strong arms. |

Here's an Image for you: New construction for Ellen and her mate, their home is all tongue and groove but no studs ......

To My Dear Girlfriend,

During the past year, I have tried to make love to you 365 times. I have succeeded 36 times, which is an average of once every ten days. The following is a list of why I did not succeed more often:

      54 times the sheets were clean

      17 times it was too late

      49 times you were too tired

      20 times it was too hot

      15 times you pretended to be asleep

      22 times you had a headache

      17 times you were afraid of waking the baby

      12 times it was the wrong time of the month

      19 times you had to get up early

      9   times you said you weren't in the mood

      7   times you were sunburned

      6   times you were watching the late show

      5   times you didn't want to mess up your new hair-do

      3   times you said the neighbors would hear us

      9   times you said your mother would hear us

Of the 36 times I did succeed, the activity was not satisfactory because:

6 times you just laid there

8 times you reminded me there's a crack in the ceiling

4 times you told me to hurry up and get it over with

7 times I had to wake you and tell you I finished

1 time I was afraid I had hurt you because I felt you move

To My Dear Boyfriend,

I think you have things a little confused. Here are the reasons you didn't get more than you did:

5 times you came home drunk and tried to screw the cat

36 times you did not come home at all

21 times you didn't cum

22 times you came too soon

19 times you went soft before you got in

38 times you worked too late

10 times you got cramps in your toes

29 times you had to get up early to play golf

2 times you were in a fight and someone kicked you in the balls

4 times you got it stuck in your zipper

3 times you had a cold and your nose was running

2 times you had a splinter in your finger

20 times you lost the notion after thinking about it all day

6 times you came in your pajamas while reading a dirty book

98 times you were too busy watching football, baseball, etc. on TV

Of the times we did get together, the reason I laid still was because: You missed and were screwing the sheets. I wasn't talking about the crack in the ceiling, what I said was, "would you prefer

me on my back or kneeling?"

Chapter XII

AND FINALLY,
THINGS THAT MAKE
YOU GO hmmmmmm ....

BULLETIN:

SENIORS ARE THE NATIONS LEADING CARRIER OF AIDS!

Hearing AIDS

Band AIDS

Roll AIDS

Walking AIDS

Medical AIDS

Government AIDS

Most of all - - - - Monetary AID to their kids!

The golden years have come at last - - -
I cannot see, I cannot pee, I cannot chew, I cannot screw.
My memory shrinks - - - my hearing stinks - - - no sense of smell - - - I look like hell!
My body is drooping - - - got trouble pooping.
The golden years have come at last - - -

THE GOLDEN YEARS CAN KISS MY ASS !

Philosophy Quiz

You don't actually have to take the quiz. Just read straight through, and you'll get the point, an awesome one, that it is trying to make!

1. Name the five wealthiest people in the world.
2. Name the last five Heisman trophy winners.
3. Name the last five winners of the Miss America contest.
4. Name ten people who have won the Nobel or Pulitzer prize.

5. Name the last half dozen Academy Award winners for best actor and actress.
6. Name the last decade's worth of World Series winners.

How did you do?

The point is, none of us remember the headliners of yesterday. These are no second-rate achievers. They are the best in their fields. But the applause dies. Awards tarnish. Achievements are forgotten. Accolades and certificates are buried with their owners.

Here's another quiz; see how you do on this one:

1. List a few teachers who aided your journey through school
2. Name three friends who have helped you through a difficult time.
3. Name five people who have taught you something worthwhile.
4. Think of a few people who have made you feel appreciated and special.
5. Think of five people you enjoy spending time with.
6. Name half a dozen heroes whose stories have inspired you.

Easier?

The lesson: the people who make a difference in your life are not the ones with the most credentials, the most money, or the most awards. They are the ones that care. Why not share this with the people who have made a difference in your life.

COW Story – 2002 Update

A CHRISTIAN DEMOCRAT: You have two cows. You keep one and give one to your neighbor, then you covet it.

A SOCIALIST: You have two cows. The government takes one and gives it to your neighbor. You form a cooperative to tell him how to manage his.

A DEMOCRAT: You have two cows; your neighbor has none. You feel guilty for being successful; you vote people into office who tax your cows, forcing you to sell one to raise money to pay the tax. The people you voted for then take the tax money and buy a cow and give it to your neighbor. You feel righteous. Barbara Streisand sings for you.

A REPUBLICAN: You have two cows, Your neighbor has none. So?

A COMMUNIST: You have two cows. The government seizes both and provides you with the milk. You wait in line for hours to get it; it is expensive and sour.

A FASCIST: You have two cows. The government seizes both and sells you the milk. You join the underground and start a campaign of sabotage, which ultimately blows up the cows.

CAPITALISM, AMERICAN STYLE: You have two cows; you sell one, buy a bull, and build a herd of cows.

DEMOCRACY, AMERICAN STYLE: You have two cows; the government taxes you to the point you have to sell both to support a man in a foreign country who has only one cow, which was a gift from your government.

BUREAUCRACY, AMERICAN STYLE: You have two cows; the government takes them both, shoots one, milks the other, pays you for the milk, and then pours the milk down the drain.

AN AMERICAN CORPORATION: You have two cows; you sell one, lease it back to yourself and do an IPO on the 2nd one. You force the 2 cows to produce the milk of four cows. You are surprised when one cow drops dead; you spin an announcement to the analysts that you have reduced your expenses. Your stock goes up.

A FRENCH CORPORATION: You have two cows; you go on strike because you want three cows. You go to lunch. Life is good.

A JAPANESE CORPORATION: You have two cows; you redesign them so they are one-tenth the size of an ordinary cow and produce twenty times the milk. They learn to travel on unbelievably crowded trains.

A GERMAN CORPORATION: You have two cows; you re-engineer them so they are all blond, drink lots of beer, give excellent quality milk, and run a hundred miles an hour. Unfortunately they also demand 13 weeks of vacation per year.

AN ITALIAN CORPORATION: You have two cows but you don't know where they are. While ambling around, you see a beautiful woman. You break for lunch; she pays for it; you spend the afternoon making love. Life is good.

A RUSSIAN CORPORATION: You have two cows; you count them and learn you have five cows. You have some more vodka; you count them again and learn you have 42 cows. You count them again and learn you have 12 cows. You stop counting cows and open another bottle of vodka. You produce your 20th 5-year plan in the last 3 months. The Mafia shows up and takes over however many cows you really have.

A SWISS CORPORATION: You have 5000 cows, none of which belong to you. You charge for storing them for others. If they give milk, you tell no one.

A TALIBAN CORPORATION: You have all the cows in Afghanistan, which is two. You don't milk them because you cannot touch any creature's private parts. At night when no one is looking, you milk both of them. Then you kill them and claim a US bomb blew them up while they were in the hospital.

A FLORIDA CORPORATION: You have a black cow and a brown cow. Everyone votes for the best looking one. Some of the people who like the brown one best vote for the black one. Some people vote for both; some people vote for neither; some people can't figure out how to vote at all. Finally, a bunch of guys from out-of-state tell you which is the best-looking one.

A NEW YORK CORPORATION: You have fifteen million cows. You have to choose which one will be the leader of the herd, so you pick some fat cow from Arkansas.

And last but not least:

ENRON VENTURE CAPITALISM: You have two cows. You sell three of them to your publicly listed company, using letters of credit opened by your brother-in-law at the bank, then execute a debt/equity swap with an associated general offer so that you get all four cows back, with a tax exemption for five cows. The milk rights of the six cows are transferred via an intermediary to a Cayman Island company secretly owned by the majority shareholder who sells the rights to all seven cows back to your listed company. The annual report says the company owns eight cows, with an option on one more.

****

Enjoy this Useless Trivia . . . . .

01) The first couple to be shown in bed together on TV: Fred and Wilma Flintstone.

02) Coca-cola was originally green.

03) Every day more money is printed for Monopoly than the US Treasury.

04) Men can read smaller print than women can; women can hear better.

05) The state with the highest percentage of people who walk to work: Alaska.

06) The percentage of Africa that is wilderness: 28%;   Now get this:

07) The percentage of North America that is wilderness: 38 %.

08) The cost of raising a medium-sized dog to the age of eleven: $6,400.

09) The average number of people airborne over the US any given hour: 61,000.

10) Intelligent people have more zinc and copper in their hair.

11) The world's youngest parents were 8 and 9 and lived in China in 1910.

12) The youngest pope was 11 years old.

13) The first novel ever written on a typewriter: Tom Sawyer.

14) Those San Francisco Cable cars are the only mobile National Monuments.

15) Each king in a deck of playing cards represents a great king from history:

Spades – King David

Hearts – Charlemagne

Clubs – Alexander the Great

Diamonds – Julius Caesar.

16) 111,111,111 x 111, 111, 111 = 12,345,678,987, 654, 321

17) If a statue in the park of a person on a horse has both front legs in the air, the person died in battle. If the horse has one front leg in the air, the person died as a result of wounds received in battle. If the horse has all four legs on the ground, the person died of natural causes.

18) Only two people signed the Declaration of Independence on July 4th, John Hancock and Charles Thomsan. Most of the rest signed on August 2, but, the last signature wasn't added until 5 years later.

19) "I am." Is the shortest complete sentence in the English language.

20) Hershey's kisses are called that because the machine that makes them looks like it's kissing the conveyor belt.

21) No NFL team which plays its home games in a domed stadium has ever won a Super Bowl.

22) The only two days of the year in which there are no professional sports game (MLB, NBA, NHL, or NFL) are the day before and the day after the Major League Baseball All-star Game.

23) How about this ....The nursery rhyme "Ring Around the Rosy" is a rhyme about the plague. Infected people with the plague would get red sores ("Ring around the rosy . . .) these, sores would smell very bad so common folks would put flowers on their bodies somewhere (inconspicuously) so that they would cover the smell of the sores (" . . . a pocket full of posies. . ."). People who died from the plague would be burned so as to reduce the possible spread of the disease ("... ashes, ashes, we all fall down!")

24) What occurs more often in December than any other month? Conception.

25) What separates "60 Minutes," on CBS from every other TV show? No theme song.

26) Half of all Americans live within 50 miles of what? Their birth-place.

27) Most boat owners name their boats. What is the most popular boat name requested? Obsession.

28) If you were to spell out numbers, how far would you have to go until you would find the letter "A"? One Thousand !

29) What do bulletproof vests, fire escapes, windshield wipers, and printers all have in common? All invented by women.

30) What is the only food that doesn't spoil? Honey.

31) There are more collect calls on this day than any other day of the year? Father's Day.

32) What trivia fact about Mel Blanc (voice of Bugs bunny) is the most ironic? He was allergic to carrots.

33) What is an activity performed by 40% of all people at a party? Snoop in your medicine cabinet.

34) In Shakespeare's time, mattresses were secured on bed frames by ropes. When you pulled on the ropes the mattress tightened, making the bed firmer to sleep on. Hence the phrase "goodnight, sleep tight".

35) It was the accepted practice in Babylon 4000 years ago that for a month after the wedding, the bride's father would supply his son-

in-law with all the mead he could drink. Mead is a honey beer and because their calendar was lunar based, this period was called the honey month or what we know today as the honeymoon.

36) In English pubs, ale is ordered by pints and quarts. So in old England, when customers got unruly, the bartender would yell at them to mind their own pints and quarts and settle down. It's where we get the phrase "mind your P's & Q's".

37) Many years ago in England, pub frequenters had a whistle baked into the rim or handle of their ceramic cups. When they needed a refill, they used the whistle to get some service. "Wet your whistle" is the phrase inspired by this practice.

38) In ancient England, a person could not have sex unless you had consent of the King (unless you were in the Royal family). When anyone wanted to have a baby, they got consent of the King, the King gave them a placard that they hung on their door while they were having sex. The placard had "F.*.*.*." (Fornication Under Consent of the King) on it. Now you know where that came from.

39) In Scotland, a new game was invented; it was entitled "Gentle-men Only, Ladies Forbidden .. " and thus the word GOLF entered into the English language.

RULE S, FACTS and QUESTIONS of LIFE

1) I can only please one person per day. Today is not your day. Tomorrow is not looking good either.

2) I love deadlines. I especially like the whooshing sound they make as they go flying by.

3) Tell me what you need, and I'll tell you how to get along without it.

4) Accept that some days you are the pigeon and some days the statue.

5) Needing someone is like needing a parachute. If he isn't there the first time, chances are you won't be needing him again.

6) I don't have an attitude problem, you have a perception problem.

7) Last night I lay in bed looking up at the stars in the sky, and I thought to myself, where the heck is the ceiling?

8) My reality check bounced.

9) On the keyboard of life, always keep one finger on the escape key.

10) I don't suffer from stress. I am a carrier.

11) You are slower than a herd of turtles stampeding through peanut butter.

12) Meddle not in the affairs of dragons, for thou art crunchy and taste good with ketchup.

13) Everybody is somebody else's weirdo.

14) Never argue with an idiot. They drag you down to their level, then beat you with experience.

15) A pat on the back is only a few centimeters from a kick in the butt.

16) Don't be irreplaceable - - if you can't be replaced, you can't be promoted.

17) You can go anywhere you want if you look serious and carry a clipboard.

18) Eat one live toad the first thing in the morning and nothing worse will happen to you the rest of the day.

19) If it wasn't for the last minutes, nothing would get done.

20) When you don't know what to do, walk fast and look worried.

21) It's always darkest before dawn, So if you're going to steal your neighbor's newspaper, that's the time to do it.

22) The journey of a thousand miles begins with a broken fan belt and a leaky tire.

23) Do not walk behind me, for I may not lead. Do not walk ahead of me, for I may not follow. Do not walk beside me, either. Just leave me the hell alone. What do I need? A restraining order?

24) Sex is like air, it's not important unless you aren't getting any.

25) No one is listening until you make a mistake.

26) Never test the depth of the water with both feet.

27) It may be that your sole purpose in life is simply to serve as a warning to others.

28) If you think nobody cares if you're alive, try missing a couple of car payments.

29) Before you criticize someone, you should walk a mile in their shoes. That way, when you criticize them, you're a mile away and you have their shoes.

30) If at first you don't succeed, skydiving is not for you.

31) Give a man a fish and he will eat for a day. Teach him how to fish and he will sit in a boat and drink beer all day.

32) If you lend someone $20.00 and never see that person again, it was probably worth it.

33) Don't squat with your spurs on.

34) If you tell the truth, you don't have to remember anything.

35) If you drink, don't park. Accidents cause people.

36) Some days you are the bug, some days you are the wind shield.

37) Don't worry, it only seems kinky the first time.

38) The quickest way to double your money is to fold it in half and put it back in your pocket.

39) Timing has an awful lot to do with the outcome of a rain dance.

40) A closed mouth gathers no foot.

41) Duct tape is like the force. It has a light side and a dark side, and it holds the universe together.

42) There are two theories to arguing with women. Neither one works.

43) Experience is something you don't get until just after you need it.

44) We are born naked, wet, and hungry. Then things get worse.

45) Don't sweat the petty things and don't pet the sweaty things.

46) One tequila, two tequila, three tequila, floor.

47) Atheism is a non-prophet organization.

48) If man evolved from monkeys and apes, why do we still have monkeys and apes?

49) The main reason Santa is so jolly is because he knows where all the bad girls live.

50) I went to a bookstore and asked the saleswoman, "where's the self-help section?" She said if she told me, it would de feat the purpose.

51) Could it be that all those trick-or-treaters wearing sheets are not going as ghosts but as mattresses?

52) If a mute swears, does his mother wash his hands with soap?

53) If a man is standing in the middle of the forest speaking and there is no woman around to hear him ... is he still wrong?

54) If someone with multiple personalities threatens to kill him self, is it considered a hostage situation?

55) Is there another word for synonym?

56) Isn't it a bit unnerving that doctors call what they do "practice"?

57) Where do forest rangers go to "get away from it all"?

58) If a parsley farmer is sued, can they garnish his wages?

59) Would a fly without wings be called a walk?

60) Why do they lock gas station bathrooms? Are they afraid someone will clean them?

61) If a turtle doesn't have a shell, is he homeless or naked?

62) Can vegetarians eat animal crackers?

63) If the police arrest a mime, do they tell him he has the right to remain silent?

64) How do blind people know when they are done wiping?

65) How do they get the deer to cross at that yellow road sign?

66) What was the best thing before sliced bread?

67) One nice thing about egotists: they don't talk about other people.

68) How is it possible to have a civil war?

69) If one synchronized swimmer drowns, do the rest drown too?

70) If you ate pasta and antipasta, would you still be hungry?

71) If you try to fail, and succeed, which have you done?

72) Whose cruel idea was it for the word "Lisp" to have an "S" in it?

73) Why is it called tourist season if we can't shoot at them?

74) Why is the alphabet in that order? Is it because of that song?

75) Why is there an expiration date on sour cream?

76) At least 5 people in this world, love you so much they would die for you.

77) At least 15 people in this world love you, in some way.

78) The only reason anyone would ever hate you, is because they want to be just like you.

79) A smile from you, can bring happiness to anyone, even if they don't like you.

80) Every night, SOMEONE thinks about you before they go to sleep.

81) You mean the world to someone.

82) Without you, someone may not be living.

83) You are special and unique, in your own way.

84) Someone that you don't know even exists, loves you.

85) When you make the biggest mistake ever, something good comes from it.

86) When you think the world has turned it's back on you, take a look; you most likely turned your back on the world.

87) When you think you have no chance at getting what you want, you probably won't get it, but if you believe in yourself, you probably sooner or later will get it.

88) Always remember compliments you received, forget about the rude remarks.

89) Always tell someone how you feel about them, you will feel much better when they know.

90) If you have a great friend, take the time to let them know that they are great.

How are you at Math?

We have all been to those meetings where someone wants over 100 percent. How about achieving 103 percent? Here's a little math that might prove helpful in the future.

What makes life 100 percent?

If "A B C D E F G H I J K L M N O P Q R S T U V W X Y Z" can be represented as

"1 2 3 4 5 6 7 8 9 10 11 12 13 14 15 16 17 18 19 20 21 22 23 24 25 26",

then

H A R D W O R K = 98 % ONLY
8 1 18 4 23 15 18 11

K N O W L E D G E = 96% ONLY
11 14 15 23 12 5 4 7 5

A T T I T U D E = 100%
1 20 20 9 20 21 4 5

B U L L S H I T = 103%
2 21 12 12 19 8 9 20

So, it stands to reason that *hardwork* and *knowledge* will get you close, but *attitude* and *bullshit* will put you over the top! ! !

WITH AGE.......COMES WISDOM!

- If you're too open minded, your brains will fall out.

- Age is a very high price to pay for maturity.

- Going to church doesn't make you a Christian any more than going to a garage makes you a mechanic.

- Artificial intelligence is not a match for natural stupidity.

- If you must choose between two evils, pick the one you've never tried before.

- My idea of housework is to sweep the room with a glance.

- Not one shred of evidence supports the notion that life is serious.

- It is easier to get forgiveness than permission.

- For every action, there is an equal and opposite government program.

- If you look like your passport picture, you probably need the trip.

- Bills travel through the mail at twice the speed of checks.

- A conscience is what hurts when all your other parts feel so good.

- Eat well, stay fit, die anyway.

- Men are from earth. Women are from earth. Deal with it.

- No husband has ever been shot while doing the dishes.

- A balanced diet is a cookie in each hand.

- Middle age is when broadness of the mind and narrowness of the waist change places.

- Opportunities always look bigger going than coming.

- Junk is something you've kept for years and throw away three weeks before you need it.

- There is always one more imbecile than you counted on.

- Experience is a wonderful thing. It enables you to recognize a mistake when you make it again.

- By the time you can make ends meet, they move the ends.

- Thou shalt not weigh more than thy refrigerator.

- Someone who thinks logically provides a nice contrast to the real world.

- Blessed are they who can laugh at themselves for they shall never cease to be amused.

REMEMBER ✳ ✳ ✳ ✳

When the worst thing you could do at school was smoke in the bathrooms, flunk a test or chew gum. And the banquets were in the cafeteria and we danced to a juke box later, and all the girls wore fluffy pastel gowns and the boys wore suits for the first time and we were allowed to stay out till 12:00 a.m.

When a '57 Chevy was everyone's dream car ... to cruise, peel out, lay rubber, and watch drag races, and people went steady and girls wore a class ring with an inch of wrapped dental floss , wax, or yarn coated with pastel frost nail polish so it would fit her finger. And no one ever asked where the car keys were 'cause they were always in the car, in the ignition, and the doors were never locked. And you got in big trouble if you accidentally locked the doors at home, since no one ever had a key.

Remember lying on your back on the grass with your friends and saying things like "That cloud looks like a ..." And playing baseball with no adults to help kids with the rules of the game. Back then, baseball was not a psychological group learning experience – it was a game.

Remember when stuff from the store came without safety caps and hermetic seals 'cause no one had yet tried to poison a perfect stranger.

And ... with all our progress ... don't you just wish .. just once .. you could slip back in time and savor the slower pace ... and share it with the children of the '80's and '90''s ......

So share these thoughts with someone who can still remember Nancy Drew, The Hardy Boys, Laurel & hardy, Howdy Doody, and The Peanut Gallery, the Lone Ranger, The Shadow Knows, Nellie Belle, Roy and Dale, Trigger and Buttermilk as well as the sound of a real mower on Saturday morning, and summers filled with bike rides, playing in cowboy land, baseball games, bowling, and visits to the pool ... and eating Kool-Aid powder with sugar. When being sent to the principal's office was nothing compared to the fate that awaited a misbehaving student at home.

Basically, we were in fear for our lives, but it wasn't because of drive by shootings, drugs, gangs, etc. Our parents and grandparents were a much bigger threat! But we all survived because their love was greater than the threat.

Now didn't that feel good, just to go back and say, Yeah, I remember that!

SIGNS 📷 📷 📷 📷 📷 SIGNS

Over a gynecologist's office: "Dr. Jones, at Your Cervix"

On a plumber's truck: "We Repair What Your Husband Fixed."

On the trucks of a local plumbing company in PA: "Don't Sleep With A Drip, Call Your Plumber"

Pizza shop slogan: "7 Days Without Pizza Makes one Weak"

Outside a muffler shop: "No Appointment Necessary . . . We hear you coming"

In a Veterinarian's Waiting Room: "Be Back in 5 minutes. Sit! Stay!"

Door of a plastic surgeon's office: "We can Help you Pick Your Nose!"

On an electrician's truck: "Let us Remove your Shorts"

In a non-smoking area:
"If we see smoke, we will assume you are on fire and take appropriate action."

On a maternity room door: "Push!   Push!   Push!"

At an optometrist's office:
"If you don't see what you're looking for, you've come to the right place."

In the front yard of a funeral home: "Drive Carefully. We'll Wait"

On the door of a Computer Store: "Out for a Quick Byte"

Outside a hotel: "Help! We need Inn-experienced People"

Outside a radiator repair shop: "Best Place in town to Take a Leak"

****

 Hello, you have reached the Psychiatric Hotline.

If you are obsessive-compulsive, press 1 repeatedly.
If you are co-dependent, get someone else to press 2.
If you have multiple personality disorder, press 3, 4, 5 and 6.
If you are schizophrenic, listen carefully and a little voice will
    tell you which
    number to press.
If you are paranoid, there is no need to press any number, we
    know who you are and what you want.

WORLD'S THINNEST BOOKS:

BOOK	AUTHOR
Staying Happily Married	Elizabeth Taylor
Beauty Secrets	Janet Reno
Home Built Appliances	John Denver
Down Hill Skiing	Sonny Bono
Atlantic Crossings of the Titanic	White Star Lines
How to Get to the Super Bowl	Dan Marino
Things I Love About Bill	Hillary Clinton
My Life's Memories	Ronald Reagan

Things I Can't Afford	Bill Gates
My Plan to Find the Real Killers	OJ Simpson
Things I would Not Do for Money	Dennis Rodman
The Wild Years	Al Gore
Guide to the Pacific Ocean	Amelia Earhart
Wild Grizzlies: Photos	Author, Unknown. .
.Disappeared	
How to Have More Patience	Anonymous Aries
How to Work Less	Workaholic Surgeon
The Joy of … Cooking ..	Unknown author
How to Make Quick Decisions	Anonymous Libra

Let's Ponder .....

If quitters never win, and winners never quit, what fool came up with "Quit while you're ahead"?

I was thinking that women should put pictures of missing husbands on beer cans.

I thought about how mothers feed their babies with little tiny spoons and forks so I wonder what Chinese mothers use. Perhaps toothpicks?

Employment application blanks always ask who is to be notified in case of an emergency. I think you should write. A good doctor.

Before they invented drawing boards, what did they go back to?

If all the world is a stage, where is the audience sitting?

If love is blind, why is lingerie so popular?

Why are hemorrhoids called "hemorrhoids? Instead of "asteroids".

If you mixed vodka with orange juice and milk of magnesia, would you get a Philip's Screwdriver?

Why do we say something is out of whack? What is a whack?

Do infants enjoy infancy as much as adults enjoy adultery?

If a pig loses its voice, is it disgruntled?

Why do women wear evening gowns to nightclubs? Shouldn't they be wearing night gowns?

When someone asks you, "A penny for your thoughts," and you put your two cents in, what happens to the other penny?

Why is the man who invests all your money called a broker?

Why do croutons come in airtight packages? It's just stale bread .

When cheese gets its picture taken, what does it say?

Why is a person who plays the piano called a pianist, but a person who drives a race car is not called a racist?

Why are a wise man and a wise guy opposites?

Why do overlook and oversee mean opposite things?

If horrific means to make horrible, does terrific mean to make terrible?

Why isn't "11" pronounced "onety-one"?

If "I am" is reported to be the shortest sentence in the English language, could it be that "I do" is the longest sentence?

If lawyers are disbarred and clergymen defrocked, doesn't it follow that electricians can be delighted, musicians denoted, cowboys deranged, models deposed, tree surgeons debarked, and dry cleaners depressed?

Do Roman paramedics refer to "IV's" as "4's" ?

Why is it that if someone tells you that there are 1 billion stars in the universe you will believe them, but if they tell you a wall has wet paint, you will have to touch it to be sure?

If you take an Oriental person and spin him around several times, does he become disoriented?

If people from Poland are called "Poles," why aren't people from Holland called "Holes" ?

☀ Cards You'll Never See in Hallmark:

Outside: Congratulations on your wedding day!
Inside: Too bad no one likes your wife.

Outside: Happy Birthday, Uncle Dad ! !
Inside: (Available only in Arkansas, Kentucky, Alabama, Maryland,
           & Tennessee)

Outside: How could two people as beautiful as you
Inside: Have such an ugly baby?

Outside: I've always wanted to have someone to hold, someone to love.
Inside: After having met you, I've changed my mind.

Outside: I must admit, you brought Religion in my life.
Inside: I never believed in Hell 'til I met you.

Outside: Looking back over the years that we've been together, I can't help but wonder:
Inside: What the f_ _k was I thinking?

Outside: As the days go by, I think of how lucky I am
Inside: That you're not here to ruin it for me.

Outside: If I get only one thing for Christmas,
Inside: I hope it's your sister.

Outside: As you grow older, Mum, I think of all the gifts you've given me.
Inside: Like the need for therapy . . . .

Outside: Thanks for being a part of my life ! ! !
Inside: I never knew what evil was before this!

Outside: Congratulations on your promotion.
Inside: Before you go, I would like you to take this knife out of my back. You'll probably need it again.

Outside: Someday I hope to get married,
Inside: But not to you.

Outside: Sorry things didn't work out,

Inside: But I can't handle guys with boobs that are bigger than mine.

Outside: Happy Birthday! You look great for your age ...
Inside: Almost lifelike!

Outside: When we were together, you always said you'd die for me.
Inside: Now that we've broken up, I think it's time you kept your promise.

Outside: I knew the day would come when you would leave me for my best friend.
Inside: So here's her leash, water bowl and chew toys.

Outside: We have been friends for a very long time,
Inside: What do you say we call it quits?

Outside: I'm so miserable without you,
Inside: It's almost like you're here.

Outside: Congratulations on your new bundle of joy.
Inside: Did you ever find out who the father is?

Outside: You are such a good friend that if we were on a sinking ship and there was only one life jacket....
Inside: I'd miss you heaps and think of you often.

Outside: Your friends and I wanted to do something special for your birthday ....
Inside: So we're having you put to sleep.

Really Interesting for Conspiracy Theorists

Subject: Creepy history – Taken from the Preface of a History book on the Two Assassinations.

Abraham Lincoln was elected to congress in 1846.
John F. Kennedy was elected to Congress in 1946.

Abraham Lincoln was elected President in 1860.
John F. Kennedy was elected President in 1960.

Both Presidents were shot on a Friday.
Both Presidents were shot in the head.

Lincoln's secretary was named Kennedy.
Kennedy's secretary was named Lincoln.

Both were succeeded by Southerners named Johnson.

Andrew Johnson, who succeeded Lincoln, was born in 1808.
Lyndon Johnson, who succeeded Kennedy, was born in 1908.

John Wilkes Booth, who assassinated Lincoln, was born in 1839.
Lee Harvey Oswald, who assassinated Kennedy, was born in 1939.

Both assassins were known by their three names.
Both names are composed of fifteen letters.

Lincoln was shot at the theater named 'Ford'.
Kennedy was shot in a car called 'Lincoln'.

Booth ran from the theater and was caught in a warehouse.
Oswald ran from a warehouse and was caught in a theater.

Booth and Oswald were assassinated before their trials.

The names Lincoln and Kennedy each contain seven letters.

Both were particularly concerned with civil rights.

Both wives lost their children while living in the White House.

Both were assassinated by Southerners.

And, here's the kicker:
A week before Lincoln was shot, he was in Monroe, Maryland.
A week before Kennedy was shot, he was with Marilyn Monroe.

8th Grade Education

With all the controversy about performance testing, I thought this was interesting.

Remember when old-timers tell us they only had an 8th grade education? Could any of us have graduated in 1895? Read on!

The following eighth-grade final exam from 1895 Salina, KS, USA was taken from the original document on file at the Smokey Valley Genealogical Society and Library in Salina, KS and reprinted by the Salina Journal.

Eighth Grade Final Exam: Salina, KS –1895

Grammar (Time, one-hour)

1. Give nine rules for the use of Capital Letters. .

2. Name the Parts of Speech and define those that have no

_____

3. Define Verse, Stanza and Paragraph.

4. What are the Principal Parts of a verb? Give Principal Parts of
   _____, _____, _____ and run.

5. Define Case, Illustrate each Case.

6. What is Punctuation? Give rules for principal marks of punctuation.

7. Write a composition of about 150 words and show therein that you understand the practical use of the rules of grammar.

Arithmetic (Time, 1.25 hours)

1. Name and define the Fundamental Rules of Arithmetic.

2. A wagon box is 2 feet deep, 10 feet long, and 3 feet wide. How many bushels of wheat will it hold?

3. If a load of wheat weighs 3942 lbs., what is it worth at 50 cents per bushel, deducting 1050 lbs for fare?

4. District No. 33 has a valuation of $35,000. What is the necessary_____ to carry on a school seven months at $50 per month and have $104 for incidentals?

5. Find cost of 6720 lbs. Coal at $6.00 per ton.

6. Find the interest of $512.60 for 8 months and 18 days at 7 percent.

7. What is the cost of 40 boards 12 inches wide and 16 ft. long at _____

8. Find bank discount on $300 for 90 days (no grace) at 10 percent.

9. What is the cost of a square farm at $15 per acre, the distance around which is 640 rods?

10. Write a Bank Check, a Promissory Note, and a Receipt.

U.S. History (Time, 45 minutes)

1.   Give the epochs into which U.S. History is divided.

2.   Give an account of the discovery of America by Columbus.

3.   Relate the causes and results of the Revolutionary War.

4.   Show the territorial growth of the United States.

5.   Tell what you can of the history of Kansas.

6.   Describe three of the most prominent battles of the Rebellion.

7.   Who were the following: Morse, Whitney, Fulton, Bell, Lincoln, Penn, and Howe?

8.   Name events connected with the following dates: 1607, 1620, 1800

Orthography (time, one hour)

1.   What is meant by the following: Alphabet, phonetic, orthography, etymology, syllabication?

2.   What are elementary sounds? How classified?

3.   What are the following, and give examples of each: Trigraph, subvocals, diphthong, cognate letters, linguals"

4.   Give four substitutes for caret 'u'.

5.   Give two rules for spelling words with final 'e'. Name two exceptions under each rule.

6.   Give two uses of silent letters in spelling. Illustrate each.

7.   Define the following prefixes and use in connection with a word: Bi, dis, mis, pre, semi, post, non, inter, mono, sup

8.   Mark diacritically and divide into syllables the following, and the sign that indicates the sound: Card, ball, mercy, sir, odd, rise, blood, fare, last.

9.   Use the following correctly in sentences, cite, site, sight, fane, fain, feign, vane, vain, vein, raze, raise, rays.

10.   Write 10 words frequently mispronounced and indicate pro nunciation by use of diacritical marks ad by syllabication.

Geography (time, one hour)

1.   What is climate? Upon what does climate depend?

2.   How do you account for the extremes of climate in Kansas?

3.   Of what use are rivers? Of what use is the ocean?

4.   Describe the mountains of North America.

5.   Name and describe the following: Monrovia, Odessa, Denver, Manitoba, Yukon, St. Helena, Juan Fernandez, Aspinwall and Orinoco.

6.   Name and locate the principal trade centers of the U.S.

7.   Name all the republics of Europe and give capital of each.

8.   Why is the Pacific Coast colder than the Atlantic in the same

_____

9.   Describe the process by which the water of the ocean re turns to _____ rivers.

10.   Describe the movements of the earth. Give inclination of the earth.

After reading this, doesn't it give a whole new meaning to an early 20th-century person saying, "I only had an 8th grade education."?!?!

ONE (1) LINERS:

- Mom's have Mother's Day, Dad's have Father's Day, what do single guys have? Palm Sunday.

- What's the difference between a Southern zoo and a Northern zoo?
A Southern zoo has a description of the animal on the front of the cage, along with a recipe.

- What's the Cuban National Anthem? "Row, Row, Row Your Boat"

- What's the difference between a Northern fairytale and a Southern fairytale?
A Northern fairytale begins "Once upon a time," and
A Southern fairytale begins "Y'all ain't gon'na believe this shit."

- Why doesn't glue stick to the inside of the bottle?

- Can fat people go skinny-dipping?

- Can you be a closet claustrophobic?

- Is it possible to be totally partial?

- If a book about failures doesn't sell, is it a success?

- If the funeral procession is at night, do folks drive with their light off?

- When companies ship styrofoam, what do they pack it in?

- If you're cross —eyed and have dyslexia, can you read all right?

- If a stealth bomber crashes in a forest, will it make a sound?

- When it rains, why don't sheep shrink?

- Do cemetery workers prefer the graveyard shift?

- What do you do when you see an endangered animal that eats only endangered plants?

- Do hungry crows have ravenous appetites?

- Why is bra plural and panties singular?

- Instead of talking to your plants, if you yelled at them would they still grow? Only to be troubled and insecure?

- When sign makers go on strike, is anything written on their signs?

- When you open a bag of cotton balls, is the top one meant to be thrown away?

- Why isn't there mouse-flavored cat food?

- Why do they report power outages on TV?

1 9 9 8 Bumper Stickers:

- Jesus is coming, everyone look busy

- A bartender is just a pharmacist with a limited inventory

- Horn broken, watch for finger

- My kid had sex with your honor student

- If at first you do succeed, try not to look astonished

- Help wanted telepath: you know where to apply

◀◀ IRS — We've got what it takes to take what you've got

◀◀ Jesus loves you - everyone else thinks you're an asshole

◀◀ I'm just driving this way to piss you off

◀◀ Reality is a crutch for people who can't handle drugs

◀◀ Keep Honking, I'm reloading

◀◀ Hang up and drive

◀◀ Lord save me from your followers

◀◀ Guns don't kill people, postal workers do

◀◀ Ask me about micro waving cats for fun and profit

◀◀ I said "no" to drugs, but they just wouldn't listen

◀◀ Friends don't let Friends drive Naked

◀◀ If we aren't supposed to eat animals, why are they made of meat?

◀◀ Lottery: A tax on people who are bad at math

◀◀ Friends help you move. Real friends help you move bodies.

◀◀ Diplomacy is the art of saying "Nice doggie!" . . . 'til you can find a rock.

◀◀ Sex on television can't hurt you, unless you fall off.

Things you wish you could say at work . . . . . .

- ☑ Ahhh...I see the f_ _ k-up fairy has visited us again . . .

- ☑ I don't know what your problem is, but I'll bet it's hard to pronounce.

- ☑ How about never?   Is never good for you?

- ☑ I see you've set aside this special time to humiliate your-self in public?

- ☑ I'm really easy to get along with once you people learn to worship me.

- ☑ I'll try being nicer if you'll try being smarter.

- ☑ I'm out of my mind, but feel free to leave a message . . .

- ☑ I don't work here, I'm a consultant

- ☑ It sounds like English, but I can't understand a word you're saying.

- ☑ I can see your point, but I still think you're full of shit.

- ☑ I like you, You remind me of when I was young and stupid.

- ☑ You are validating my inherent mistrust of strangers.

- ☑ I have plenty of talent and vision. I just don't give a damn.

- ☑ I'm already visualizing the duct tape over your mouth.

- ☑ I will always cherish the initial misconceptions I had about you.

☑ Thank you. We're all refreshed and challenged by your unique point of view.

☑ The fact that no one understands you doesn't mean you're an artist.

☑ Any connection between your reality and mine is purely coincidental.

☑ What am I? Flypaper for freaks!?

☑ I'm not being rude. You're just insignificant.

☑ It's a thankless job, but I've got a lot of Karma to burn off.

☑ Yes, I am an agent of Satan, but my duties are largely ceremonial.

☑ No my powers can only be used for good.

☑ You sound reasonable ... Time to up the medication.

☑ Who me? I just wander from room to room.

Talk About Putting it all in Perspective

You think a gallon of gasoline is expensive, Huh ? ?; consider the following:

Diet Snapple 16oz for $1.29 = $10.32 per gallon

Lipton Ice Tea 16 oz for $1.19 = $9.52 per gallon

Gatorade 20 oz for $1.59 = $10.17 per gallon

Ocean Spray 16 oz for $1.25 = $10.00 per gallon

Pint of Milk 16 oz for $1.59 = $12.72 per gallon

STP Brake Fluid 12 oz for $3.15 = $dd.60 per gallon

Vick's Nyquil 6 oz for $8.35 = $178.13 per gallon

Pepto Bismol 4 oz for $3.85 = $123.20 per gallon

Scope 1.5 oz for $.99 = $84.48 per gallon

Evian Water 9oz for $1.49 = $21.19 per gallon
.......**$21.19 for WATER ! ! !**

So next time you're at the pump, be glad your car doesn't run on Nyquil, or Scope, or Water !

Now that I am older, here's what I have discovered:

My wild oats have turned into prunes and All Bran.

I finally got my head together, now my body is falling apart.

Funny, I don't remember being absent minded . . . .

All reports are in; Life is now officially unfair.

If all is not lost, where is it?

It is easier to get older than it is to get wiser.

Some days you're the dog; some days you're the hydrant.

I wish the buck stopped here; I sure could use a few ...

Kids in the back seat cause accidents.

Accidents in the back seat cause kids.

It's hard to make a comeback when you haven't been anywhere.

Only time the world beats a path to your door is when
you're in the bathroom.

If God wanted me to touch my toes, he would have put
them on my knees ..

When I'm finally holding all the cards, why does everyone
decide to play chess?

It's not hard to meet expenses – they're everywhere!

The only difference between a rut and a grave is the depth.

These days I spend a lot of time thinking about the hereaf-
ter ... I go somewhere to get something, and then
wonder what I'm here after!

And you know you're getting old when:

Your potted plants stay alive.

Having sex in a twin-sized bed is absurd.

You keep more food than beer in the fridge.

6:00 a.m. is when you get up, not when you go to sleep.

You hear your favorite song on the elevator at work.

You carry an umbrella.

You watch the Weather Channel.

Your friends marry and divorce instead of hook-up and break-up.
You go from 130 days of vacation time to 7.

Jeans and a sweater no longer qualify as 'dressed up'.

You're the one calling the police because those damn kids next door don't know how to turn down the stereo.

Older relatives feel comfortable telling sex jokes around you.

You don't know what time Taco Bell closes anymore.

Your car insurance goes down and your car payments go up.

You feed your dog Science Diet instead of McDonalds.

Sleeping on the couch is a no-no.

You no longer take naps from noon to 6:00 p.m.

MTV News is no longer your primary source for information.

You go to the drugstore for Ibuprofen and antacids, not condoms and pregnancy test kits.

A $4.00 bottle of wine is no longer 'pretty good stuff'.

You actually eat breakfast foods at breakfast time.

Grocery lists are longer than macaroni and cheese, diet Pepsi, and Ho-Ho's.

You don't get liquored up at home, to save money, before going to the bar.

ONLY IN AMERICA . . . .

......can a pizza get to your house faster than an ambulance.

......are there handicap parking places in front of a skating rink.

......do drugstores make the sick walk all the way to the back of the store to get their prescriptions.

......do people order double cheese burgers, a large fries, and a diet coke!

......do banks leave their front and back doors open and then chain the pens to the counters.

......do we leave cars worth thousands of dollars in the driveway and leave useless junk in the garage.

......do we buy hot dogs in packages of ten and buns in packages of eight.

......do we use answering machines to screen calls and then have 'call waiting' so we won't miss a call from someone we didn't want to talk to in the first place.

......do we use the word 'politics' to describe the process so well: "Poli" in Latin meaning "many" and "tics" meaning "blood sucking creatures".

Sayings for any Occasion

Make yourself at home! Clean my kitchen.

Well, aren't we just a ray of f_ _ _ing sunshine?

A hard-on doesn't count as personal growth.

Don't bother me. I'm living happily ever after.

Do I look like a F_ _king people person?

This isn't an office; it's hell with fluorescent lighting.

I started out with nothing and still have most of it left.

I pretend to work; they pretend to pay me.

Therapy is expensive, poppin' bubble wrap is cheap! You choose!

Practice random acts of intelligence and senseless acts of self-control.

If I want to hear the pitter-patter of little feet, I'll put shoes on my cat.

Did the aliens forget to remove your anal probe?

I wish for a world of peace, harmony, and nakedness.

Let me show you how the guards used to do it.

See no evil, hear no evil, date no evil.

Whisper my favorite words: "I'll buy it for you."

Better living through denial.

Suburbia: where they tear out the trees and then name streets after them.

Do theyever shut up on your planet?

Are those your eyeballs? I found them in my cleavage.

I'm not your type. I'm not inflatable.

A cubicle is just a padded cell without a door.

Here I am! Now what are your other two wishes?

Back off! You're standing in my aura.

Don't worry, I forgot your name, too!

One of us is thinking about sex ... OK, it's me.

It's sick the way you people keep having sex without me.

I work 40 hours a week to be this poor.

Okay, okay, I take it back! UnF_ _ k you!

Macho Law forbids me from admitting I'm wrong.

Not all men are annoying, Some are dead.

Too many freaks, not enough circuses.

Other Ponderings:

❖ What is the speed of dark?

❖ Why are there Braille signs on drive up ATMs?

❖ If women wear a pair of pants, a pair of glasses, and a pair of earrings, why don't they wear a pair of bras?

❖ How come you never hear about gruntled employees?

❖ What is a "free" gift? Aren't all gifts free?

❖ After eating, do amphibians have to wait one hour before getting out of the water?

❖ If white wine goes with fish, do white grapes go with sushi?

❖ Why are builders afraid to have a 13th floor but book publishers aren't afraid to have a Chapter 11?

❖ How can there be self-help groups?

❖ Why do you need a driver's license to buy liquor when you can't drink and drive?

❖ Why are cigarettes sold in gas stations when smoking is prohibited there?

❖ If a cow laughed, would milk come out her nose?

❖ Why are there interstate highways in Hawaii?

❖ Why is it that when you transport something by car, it's called a shipment, but when you transport something by ship, its called cargo?

❖ Why isn't phonetic spelled the way it sounds?

❖ Are there seeing eye humans for blind dogs?

❖ If knees were backwards, what would chairs look like?

❖ When your pet bird sees you reading the newspaper, does he wonder why you're just sitting there, staring at carpeting?

❖ If an orange is orange, why isn't a lime called a green or a lemon called a yellow?

❖ Why does your nose run and your feet smell?

❖ If olive oil comes from olives, where does baby oil come from?

❖ There's a fine line between fishing and just standing on the shore like an idiot.

❖ How much deeper would the ocean be if sponges didn't live there?

❖ The other day I went to a tourist information booth and asked, "Tell me about some of the people who were here last year."

❖ What a nice night for an evening.

❖ When I was in high school, I got in trouble with my girlfriend's Dad. He said, "I want my daughter back by 8:15." I said, "the middle of August? Cool!"

❖ Did Washington just flash a quarter for his ID?

❖ I just got skylights put in my place; the people who live above me are furious.

❖ I live on a one-way dead-end street.

❖ It doesn't matter what temperature a room is, it's always room temperature.

❖ Yesterday, my eyeglass prescription ran out.

❖ I was hitchhiking the other day and a hearse stopped. I said, "No thanks, I'm not going that far."

❖ I played a blank tape on full volume. The mime who lives next door complained.

❖ Why in a country of free speech, are there phone bills.

❖ When a man talks dirty to a woman, it's sexual harassment. When a woman talks dirty to a man, it's $3.95 per minute.

❖ Why do we play in recitals and recite in plays?

❖ Where are Preparations A through G?

❖ My school colors were "clear".

❖ I stayed in a really old hotel last night. They sent me a wake up letter.

❖ I'm taking Lamaze classes. I'm not having a baby, I'm just having trouble breathing.

❖ My girlfriend is weird. She asked me "If you could know how and when you were going to die, would you want to know?" I said, "No". She said, "Okay, then forget it."

❖ I went for a walk last night and she asked me how long I was going to be gone. I said "the whole time".

❖ Hermits have no peer pressure.

❖ Whenever I think of the past, it brings back so many memories!

I've Learned ...

I've learned- That you cannot make someone love you. All you can do is be someone who can be loved. The rest is up to them.

I've learned- That no matter how much I care, some people just don't care back.

I've learned- That it takes years to build up trust, and only seconds to destroy it.

I've learned- That it's not what you have in your life, but who you have in your life that counts.

I've learned- That you can get by on charm for about fifteen minutes.

I've learned- After that, you'd better know something.

I've learned- That you shouldn't compare yourself to the best others can do.

I've learned- That you can do something in an instant that will give you heartache for life.

I've learned- That it's taking me a long time to become the person I want to be.

I've learned- That you should always leave loved ones with loving words. It may be the last time you see them.

I've learned- That you can keep going long after you can't.

I've learned- That we are responsible for what we do, no matter how we feel.

I've learned- That either you control your attitude or it controls you.

I've learned- That regardless of how hot and steamy a relationship is at first, the passion fades and there had better be something else to take its place.

I've learned- That heroes are the people who do what has to be done when it needs to be done, regardless of the consequences.

I've learned- That money is a lousy way of keeping score.

I've learned- That my best friend and I can do anything or nothing and have the best time.

I've learned- That sometimes the people you expect to kick you when you're down, will be the ones to help you get back up.

I've learned- That sometimes when I'm angry, I have the right to be angry, but that doesn't give me the right to be cruel.

I've learned- That true friendship continues to grow, even over the longest distance. Same goes for true love.

I've learned- That just because someone doesn't love you the way you want them to doesn't mean they don't love you with all they have.

I've learned- That maturity has more to do with what types of experiences you've had and what you've learned from them and less to do with how many birthdays you've celebrated.

I've learned- That you should never tell a child their dreams are unlikely or outlandish. Few things are more humiliating, and what a tragedy it would be if they believed it.

I've learned- That your family won't always be there for you. It may seem funny, but people you aren't related to can take care of you and love you and teach you to trust people again. Families aren't biological.

I've learned- That no matter how good a friend is, they're going to hurt you every once in a while and you must forgive them for that.

I've learned- That it isn't always enough to be forgiven by others. Sometimes you are to learn to forgive yourself.

I've learned- That no matter how bad your heart is broken the world doesn't stop for your grief.

I've learned- That our background and circumstances may have influenced who we are, but we are responsible for who we become.

I've learned- That just because two people argue, it doesn't mean they don't love each other. And just because they don't argue, it doesn't mean they do.

I've learned- That we don't have to change friends if we under stand that friends change.

I've learned- That you shouldn't be so eager to find out a secret. It could change your life forever.

I've learned- That two people can look at the exact same thing and see something totally different.

I've learned- That no matter how you try to protect your children, they will eventually get hurt and you will hurt in the process.

I've learned- That your life can be changed in a matter of hours by people who don't even know you.

I've learned- That even when you think you have no more to give, when a friend cries out to you, you will find the strength to help.

I've learned- That credentials on the wall do not make you a decent human being.

I've learned- That the people you care about most in life are taken from you too soon.

I've learned- That it's hard to determine where to draw the line between being nice and not hurting people's feelings and standing up for what you believe.

8/2/16 12/15/14 20

Printed in the United States
1477600004B/52-255